Praise fo

'What is most appealing ab
unpretentiousness, combine
the follies of contemporary life'
THE TIMES

'The one thing Bennett can't pretend to be useless at is
writing – his deadpan style is sharp enough to win you over'
BIG ISSUE

'He is still the grand master, the alchemist of words. No
wonder Bill Bryson has pronounced him brilliant. These
pieces are beautifully written, hilarious, shrewd and
illuminating'
THE PRESS

'Excellent, excellent, excellent . . . Joe Bennett's use of
language is legendary . . . And he's funny. That's the icing.
The hardest thing about this book will be beating back the
friends who want to "borrow" it'
THE NELSON MAIL

'Infused with a sense of childlike wonder and understated
bonhomie. He has the columnist's keen eye for minutiae and
a gentle way of inpeeling the complexities of daily dilemmas
to reveal the absurdity beneath'
WAIKATO TIMES

'He is that rare thing, a thoughtful and good-natured
humorist, and his pieces have a value beyond the occasions
that prompt them'
NEW ZEALAND LISTENER

'Utterly enjoyable'
NEW ZEALAND HERALD

Joe Bennett was born in Eastbourne and since leaving Cambridge University has taught English in a variety of countries including Canada, Spain and New Zealand. Scribner published his first collection of essays, *Fun Run and Other Oxymorons*, in 2000. He lives in Christchurch, New Zealand.

Bedside Lovers (and Other Goats)

Joe Bennett

Scribner

First Published in Great Britain by Scribner, 2002
An imprint of Simon & Schuster UK Ltd
A Viacom Company

Copyright © Joe Bennett, 2002
Most articles in this book have been previously published in
New Zealand in two books, *Sit* and *So Help Me Dog*, both
published by Hazard Press.

This book is copyright under the Berne Convention
No reproduction without permission
® and © 1997 Simon & Schuster Inc. all rights reserved.

Scribner and design are trademarks of Macmillan Library
Reference USA, Inc., used under licence by Simon & Schuster,
the publisher of this work.

The right of Joe Bennett to be identified as author of this work
has been asserted by him in accordance with sections 77 and 78
of the Copyright, Designs and Patents Act, 1988.

1 3 5 7 9 10 8 6 4 2

Simon & Schuster UK Ltd
Africa House
64–78 Kingsway
London WC2B 6AH

www.simonsays.co.uk

Simon & Schuster Australia
Sydney

A CIP Catalogue for this book is available from the British Library

ISBN 0-7432-1997-X

Typeset in Sabon by SX Composing DTP, Rayleigh, Essex
Printed and bound in Great Britain by
Omnia Books Limited, Glasgow

Contents

Foreword

My last book had a foreword but didn't need it. This book doesn't need one either so here it is.

The presence of a foreword implies a plan. This book has no plan. If the pages that follow suggest a coherent view of the world I shall be surprised. Coherent views of the world are nice but nonsense.

J.B., Lyttelton, New Zealand

In the bad lands

It rose in front of us, sheer, gaunt and majestic. I gasped. Pete gulped. Side by side we stood to gasp and gulp in wonder. Much had we travelled in the realms of cliché but never had we seen so steep a learning curve.

In comparison with this awesome steepness, every other peak that Pete and I had climbed seemed little more than a level playing field.

We knew immediately that we had no choice. Before us stood the ultimate challenge, our new mission statement. We would tackle this learning curve head on. We would put our noses to the grindstone till they bled. Nothing would stand in the way of our ascent.

'Enjoy,' said Pete with a wry grim smile.

'Enjoy what?' I asked, but he was already away.

Up we plodded, step after laborious step, pausing occasionally to look around us. We knew what we were looking for. We sought a window of opportunity, just a small one that would grant a view of the knowledge economy from the top of the learning curve. But windows of opportunity are few and far between and the going was tough.

Obstacles abounded. We waded through income streams and held each other back from cunningly concealed poverty traps.

After twenty-four hours we were on the point of calling it a day when Pete clasped my shoulder.

'Look,' he said.

I looked. On the slope ahead of us, miraculously it seemed, stood a small city square, immaculate with cafés and bars and colonnades. We sank gratefully down at a café table, ordered refreshments from the waitperson and applied ourselves to the problems that faced us. But hard though we thought, no ideas came. Then silently Pete rose and went to stand beyond the furthest building, his chin cupped in his hand. Almost immediately he yelped with delight.

I ran to join him.

'I've got it,' he exclaimed.

'Ah,' I said as the truth dawned on me, 'of course, thinking outside the square. Why didn't I think of that?'

'Never mind that,' said Pete. 'Look!'

I looked and beheld a sight I shall never forget as long as I remember it. There stood the window that we sought and oh what light through yonder window broke. It was the light of opportunity. Without another word Pete and I ran to it, fumbled frantically with the catch, threw open the window and beheld spread out before us . . . but the story is almost too sad to tell. Our hopes were dashed. They lay in tatters round our ankles. There seemed no point in hauling them back up.

For where we had expected to see the verdant fields of a knowledge economy, or at least the pleasant pastures of a win-win situation, we beheld nothing more and nothing less than the smoking rubble of a worst-case scenario. It was almost too much to bear.

I looked at Pete. Pete looked at me. It would not be stretching a point to say we looked at each other. Despair was etched on our faces. Horror was tattooed on our chests. Hopelessness was scribbled on our thighs. There was nothing for it. We had only one card left to play and we played it.

Pete reinvented the wheel. Instantly I put my shoulder to it, but Pete pulled me roughly away, reinvented another wheel, attached the two of them to a bicycle frame that he had also reinvented and together we pedalled back down the learning curve as if the devil were after us. I looked over my shoulder. The devil was after us.

'Faster,' I screamed. Downwards we flew, past the lowest common denominators who backed away in fear, past the level playing field where someone was moving the goalposts, back towards the sanctuary of the old economy when, without warning, a vehicle appeared in front of us with flashing lights and blaring siren. We were going too fast to stop and we crashed slap bang into the ambulance at the foot of the cliff.

Pete was thrown from the bike, performed a double somersault and a single dead-cat bounce then lay as still as stone.

'A health professional, a health professional,' I

screamed, 'my kingdom for a health professional.' I rushed to Pete's side and cradled his head in my hands.

'Pete, Pete,' I whispered urgently, 'use your communication skills to me.'

But it was no good. Pete's window of opportunity had closed for ever. He had reached his bottom line.

Ahoy

When I was a kid there were lots of words I couldn't spell, but only two I knew I couldn't spell. I can spell them now, of course, but I still remember the confusion they caused me. One was Egypt and the other was yot.

The dictionary I intend to write defines a yot as 'a stationary possession disguised as a mode of transport, occupied by a fool, and bounded on one side by water and on the other by a berth priced at the GDP of Belgium'. The same dictionary defines Egypt as a hot place I haven't visited.

Much have I travelled in the realms of gold, and, I would add, many goodly states and kingdoms seen, but I have never been tempted by Egypt. Of Egypt I know only the pyramids and I don't understand them. I believe none of the nonsense about their being used for astronomical calculation, and as domestic architecture they're disastrous. I'd rather die than live in one.

Cleopatra was a famous Egyptian. President Nasser was the other one. By a curious coincidence, Cleopatra happened to be the world's first yotsperson. Shakespeare described her yot as a barge, but he was in love with Tom Stoppard at the time and preoccupied with a screenplay. A yot it was, and like a burnished throne for that matter, with a couple of pyramids in the fo'c'sle (pronounced forecastle) as a sort of sextant. President Nasser was not a yotsperson, but the Americans still named their space agency after him in the hope of flattering him into telling them the astronomical secrets of the pyramids.

So, as you can see, I'm up to speed with yots and yotting, the history, practice and navigation thereof, so when a close neighbour and distant friend of mine who has often expressed an urge to keelhaul my dogs, invited me out for a quick schmozzle round Lyttelton Harbour on his spanking new 36-footer it was the work of a moment for me to hide under the house.

But he's not the sort of fellow to let seaweed grow under his feet, and before you could say 'hoist the mains'l' I found myself down at what we old sea dogs call the edge of the water, dressed for the voyage in an oilskin and a rather fetching blue funk. The old salt invited me aboard by pushing me off the jetty. He then suggested I earn my keep by hauling on the painter and weighing the anchor. The painter seemed to have withdrawn to the pub but I resisted the urge to join him by skilfully inserting the tail of my oilskin into the captain's hands while pretending to climb ashore.

Pausing only to toss my will to a passing cormorant, I signalled to the skipper that all was shipshape under the mizzen and we cast off.

Suddenly we were at sea, with only a skin of fibreglass between me and the ravening dolphins, and as the deck pitched beneath my feet I felt that exhilaration that makes us yotties yot.

Driven to express my exhilaration I headed for the heads (pronounced poopdeck), where I found my sea legs, screwed them on and was back on deck in a trice (pronounced two and a half hours). Aloft once more and feeling chipper as a corpse, I trimmed the gymbals, spliced the spinnaker, braced the bowsprit and made a suggestion. 'Let me off,' I suggested in the measured tone of a spoilt three-year-old.

From the discomfort of his air-conditioned wheelhouse the old sea dog was all sympathy. 'Prepare to tack, me hearty,' he bellowed into the teeth of the gale which swallowed his words at a gulp and grinned for more, 'going about'.

There is a merry little thing on board all yots called the boom. It's a sort of two-ton scythe. The entertaining purpose of a boom is to catch us tars on the back of the skull, but I am too tarry a tar to fall for the boom-in-the-back-of-the-head trick. As we yawled our gunwales to windward I sensed the boom's approach and turned just in time to catch it neatly on the right temple.

After briefly pondering the range of options available to me, I chose to lose consciousness. It is an old truth of the sea that the pleasures of yotting increase in direct proportion to the degree of coma. When I came to, we were dibbling back into the marina. Masking my disappointment with a chorus of 'yessirree' and a celebratory jig round a main-sheet (pronounced rope), I leapt ashore.

'Leapt' is precisely the right verb. 'Ashore' is about half a metre away from being the right adverb.

'Ho ho,' sympathized the old sea dog. I bade him a cheerful farewell with the gesture known to yotties as Cleopatra's Needle and went home (pronounced home).

The squeals of children

The hills are alive with the squeals of children. I've got a cageful of the little darlings all pleading for forgiveness, having dared to approach my battlements last week in their capes and plastic teeth squeaking trick or treat in bogus American accents. Well, they got the trick and I got the treat and the dogs are still fetching in the stragglers. Not much warmth in those tinsel capes either, as the honeys are discovering these cool spring nights.

'Let us out, mister,' they whine as I curl up on the rococo sofa smug with whisky, 'we didn't mean no harm.'

Nor did I, as it happened, it just sort of turned out that way. Not that I haven't given them the chance of redemption. 'Tell me the historical and religious significance of Hallowe'en,' I said, 'and all will be forgiven.' They shrugged what pass for shoulders.

Same thing happened to the Guy Fawkes mob last weekend. 'Penny for the guy,' they squeaked over a pramful of straw. Well, that was enough for me. Now they're all locked in the garage, howling like banshees while I toss an occasional cheap firework through the window. They'll be there till they give me a decent biographical summary of Mr Fawkes or at least an explanation of imperial currency. To give them a chance I even slid an encyclopedia through the grating, but most of the little sods couldn't read a word, and the only one who could looked up Guy Fawkes under cutlery.

Nice to turn the tables on the tyranny of youth. Not that it's all their fault of course. About ten years old, most of them, ten years of advertising, television, video games and the Spice Girls, so it's hardly surprising they're as ignorant as suet. As for any sense of historical perspective or the reasons for ritual, you might as well go scraping round for poets in the Stock Exchange.

And did you listen to the outcry over Hallowe'en? 'Oh gosh,' say the adults, 'it's just another ghastly American import.' Well pfui to that for a start. Mother's Day, Father's Day, where do they come from? 'Oh,' we say, 'but it's so commercial', we who do a third of our annual retail spending for the great religious bash of Christmas, which is a nice little import from the Middle East, that notorious bastion of peace and goodwill to all men. Add a wallop of paganism and Teutonic solstice-worship and a plastic Christmas tree and things that unfurl and go toot when you blow in them and then we have a real cultural event of symbolic significance. But the kiddies can't have one of their own. Oh no, Hallowe'en is sending out all the wrong signals.

The wrong signals? Surely it's sending out all the right signals. Spend money, make the economy boom, chisel as much as you can out of the old, weak and housebound, by terror if necessary, con the populace into paying for shoddiness, surely these are better and more realistic lessons than they've had in school for many a long year. That's the society they're being groomed for and then we moan when they turn out like us.

No, if you want to do something about the little buggers turning out wrong you've got a couple of choices. One, of course, is to biff a brick through the telly, sell all shares in The Warehouse and go back to singing hymns round the piano with the servants and a roomful of family values.

The other way is my way and it's much more fun. Try beating the little darlings into submission. The cult of the child has gone on far too long. The quaint eighteenth-century idea that they're all little angels whose self-esteem has been devastated by the traumas of industrial society got well and truly exploded in the French Revolution and at roughly fifty-year intervals ever since. But the whole of our current education system is founded on that mischievous little myth and look where it's got us: tides of ignorance seeping under the skirting boards. No, far better to presume that the tinies are born twisted and all need straightening out to some degree or other, which is a far older notion known as the fall of man and which makes a sight more sense when you're faced with the reality of a classroom full of the little loves.

Once bitten twice shy, so bite them. They don't come back. My Hallowe'en next year will be as peaceful as All Saints Day. And there's an idea. All Saints Day – what a marketing opportunity. Think of the merchandising, think of the slogans. Those saints were good guys. They'll be a doddle to sell.

Gone goat

Don't look over your shoulder. It brings only grief. For behind us lies the land of might-have-been, irrecoverable, receding into the distance as the steamboat of time carries us out into the ocean of nonentity. The coastline of might-have-been becomes a smudge on the horizon then fades for ever into the limitless nowhere of the sea of middle-class middle age. It is profoundly sad.

Such potential we had when we were young. Where did it go? For sure it has gone, faded like smoke, melded indistinguishably into the bland air, and all our dreams gone with it.

When I look back I see a seven-year-old at a party. That boy was me and back then I knew stuff. I knew that life was a game of sheep and goats and I wanted to be on the side of whichever animal it was that won. On balance I fancied the goats. I still do. They have better horns, better digestive systems and they eat washing.

The party was thrown by a fat boy to indulge his gluttony, and we all duly trooped along to glut with him and to play pass-the-parcel. I could glut with the best of them but I was better still at pass-the-parcel. I cheated. I seized the parcel from girls before my turn. I hung on to it longer than I should. I tore at its wrappings with my teeth. There was a prize inside that parcel and I meant it to be mine. I was raw goat.

I won, of course. The prize came in a little box. I opened the box and found it empty. The prize was the box. But though the box had nothing inside it, I did. I had greed. I was goat. The goat burst into tears.

I hunted down the fat boy's fat mother and I wailed. She said the box was a nice box and that was that. She went away. I followed her. I followed her like a goat after washing. I wanted a better prize. Whenever the fat mother turned she tripped over a seven-year-old in tears and Marks and Spencer sandals. With my undissuadable mix of persistence and emotional manipulation I wore her down. She gave me a different prize. I have forgotten what it was.

But I haven't forgotten the attitude. If only I had retained such tenacity. But it has gone, all gone. Today, crippled by fear, and an outmoded sense of courtesy and the needs of others and the wish to avoid a scene, I take what I am given. Today I would be more likely to say, 'Oh no, don't bother. Actually I rather like the empty box. It is, if you like, a sort of metaphor for the hollowness of mere acquisition, a cross between a *caveat emptor* and a *memento mori* for the consumer society, don't you think? Indeed it is by far the best prize I have ever won. I am thrilled by my empty box. Please don't trouble yourself in the least about finding a substitute prize. I could hardly be closer to ecstasy. I say, what wonderful wallpaper. Did you stencil it yourself?'

The years have taught me to lie. Back then I was all innocent honesty. Give, I said, and meant it, and stuck with it, barren of rhetoric, devoid of politesse. I was goat, all emphatic, imperative greed, and wholly admirable. And it worked. Contrary to all the pious nonsense of grandma and other defeated adults, he who asks does get, and he goes on getting and getting until he dies with a houseful of pass-the-parcel prizes in Parnell.

What could I not have done? With that rapacity and single-minded devotion to self I could have been a chisel-faced banker. I could have cut deals and screwed the opposition, and trodden on fingers and found venture capital and been knighted for services to myself. I could have animated advertisements for breakfast cereals. I could have talked glibly of quality-driven, client-focused synergy and pocketed the dosh. I could have gone drinking with Vince Lombardi and when he said 'Winning isn't everything – it's the only thing', I could have slapped him on the back and ordered another highball. I could have reaped the harvest of greed and manipulation and all the other virtues that society rewards while it pretends to despise them. I could have inherited the earth. Oh it would have been wonderful. But instead I got meek.

Where did I go wrong? Where is my goat of yesteryear? Gone, long gone. Too late, old boy, the saddest words in the English language.

Aubergine therapy

Until recently I knew little about modern medicine.
I was a robust child and I met my doctor only three
times. The first was when he attended my birth but
I ignored him. I was too intent, at the time, on
launching my lifelong career in bawling for
attention.

I didn't meet my doctor properly until I was
eight. That was when I caught my foreskin in the
zip of my trousers. I found it impossible to tell my
mother what had happened, so I told my brother.
He found it impossible not to tell my mother and
everyone else in the neighbourhood. Soon afterwards the doctor arrived in my bedroom clutching
a large pair of boltcutters. As it turned out, the
boltcutters were not required and the doctor fixed
the problem with decisive swiftness once my
mother had peeled me from the ceiling.

The only other time I met the doctor I brought
him an ankle like an aubergine. I had twisted it
playing soccer and I believed it broken. The doctor
twisted it some more in a manner which I found
most amusing and then told me an X-ray was
unnecessary, that time would work its recuperative

wonder and that I would be playing soccer again in three weeks. I was.

Earlier this year I twisted my other ankle. I sustained the injury on the squash court rather than the soccer pitch, but the acute pain and the decorative effect were identical. And after a session in the surgery which reminded me of all the fun of thirty years before, the doctor pronounced that the ankle required a course of physiotherapy.

Now I may have known little about conventional medicine but I knew even less about physiotherapy. I knew that, like consultancy, it was a boom industry of the nineties, but otherwise I bracketed it vaguely with all the other therapies – psycho, aroma, retail and so on. My only connection with these, and a tenuous one at best, was that I call the starter cord on my lawnmower 'the chiropractor' because it is unlikely to do any good to my back.

If pressed I would have said that physiotherapy involved vigorous wrenching and bending and my first sight of Mr Physio confirmed that idea. He wore I'm-healthy shorts and bore that scrawny, muscular look of the dedicated mountain-biker which is so often mistaken for sanity. But he neither wrenched nor bent me. He used gadgets.

First he smeared me with erotic gel, then he rubbed my ankle with a blunt instrument. It seemed to promise much but I felt nothing. Mr Physio explained that this was ultrasound, a sort of inaudible Lite FM. Apparently it soothes troubled muscles by singing to them at a pitch that is popular with bats.

Having soothed the leg he then tortured it. Acupuncture works on the principle that a needle stuck into one place will affect a different place. So, I believe, does voodoo.

'You may feel a slight tingling,' said the physio-therapist. I didn't feel a slight tingling. I felt a needle going into my knee. Bleeding was minimal, however, and I enjoyed the process in much the same way as an athletics official enjoys visiting A & E wearing a javelin.

The third stage of my treatment featured a close relative of the machine which they used to apply to the heads of schizophrenics. The physio taped electrodes to my ankle and zapped me. And having instructed me to turn the dial to any level that I found comfortable, he left to zap someone else.

The level that I found comfortable was zero. But the man on the next bed was undergoing the same treatment and the urge to compete beats strongly in the male chest. When the physio returned, both of us were humming like tuning forks. I was three volts away from the recommended dose for murderers in Florida.

I returned in the days that followed for two more sessions of physio. Gradually the swelling subsided, the aubergine faded, the muscles recovered and I returned to the squash court. And, most remarkable of all, it took precisely three weeks.

I believe in pigs

A pig's orgasm lasts for half an hour.

I learned this splendid nugget a couple of weeks ago and it has since become a fixture in my conversational repertoire. It sparks a lively response at any social event but is best reserved for formal dinner parties. It goes down well with loin of pork.

I learned about the pig from Pat, a music teacher who has never, to my knowledge or suspicion, been in a position to verify the truth of his assertion. But that doesn't stop me believing it. The nub of the matter is not that I think it is true, but that I want it to be true.

There is probably a word for this tendency of mine, but I suspect it is a Greek word and I'm afraid all Greek is Greek to me. The word I'm looking for isn't stupidity and it isn't credulousness. I want a word to describe something altogether more wilful which has been the mainstay of my intellectual life. I want a word to describe the tendency of human beings to prefer the excitingly improbable idea to the dull and more probable one.

Why is it, for example, that for thirty years or so

I have believed that glass is a liquid? It looks and feels like a solid, it sounds like a solid when I tap it, when I tap it too hard it slices my flesh and yet I have told innumerable people that it is a liquid and for evidence I have pointed out that ancient windows are thicker at the bottom than at the top because, over the course of the centuries, the glass has slowly dripped. Obviously, I have never examined ancient windows to see if it is so, but someone whom I can no longer remember once told me it was so and it sounded exciting to me and so I decided it was so.

And while I am at it, why should I and so many other people have believed that powdered glass in coffee is a recognized method of murder? Powdered glass in coffee would settle as sludge at the bottom of the cup and the victim would have to spoon the murder weapon down his throat himself. And even if he did so the glass would pass harmlessly though his gut. Nevertheless for years I have believed the irrational exciting opposite of the truth.

Just as when people come across flattened wheat they presume not that wind has laid it low nor that people or animals have trodden it down but that aliens have travelled hundreds of light years across the galaxy in order to crush a fraction of a cereal crop before going home. And how we all would like it to be true.

And why, when a friend is late for a meeting, do I always imagine that something disastrous has happened, that a car crash has left him mangled in a ditch? And if I am alone in a house at night why, when I hear a noise, do I assume that it is not a possum on the roof or a creak in the weatherboards but rather an intruder with a baseball bat and malice, or a ghost with the face of a skull, so that I withdraw whimpering beneath the blankets?

And why, when probability theory tells the plainest story of folly, do a million people troop to the Lotto shop every Saturday to hand over the money that they love in the strange conviction that they have been singled out?

And why do people who know that we live in a galaxy of cooling lumps of matter circling other cooling lumps of matter cling to the belief, the hope, that destiny is written in the heavens, that the orbit of the planets somehow impinges on the fate of each of us?

And why, when Elvis is dead, for which relief much thanks, should he reappear so frequently in the supermarkets of Tennessee?

Why should these and a thousand other superstitions, myths and fallacies so grasp our minds? For sure the wish is father to the thought but why should the wish exist? Why should we want the world to be more than it is, to offer greater delights, stranger truths, greater mysteries? Could it be that the miraculous truth of life is essentially a mundane miracle and we cannot accept that dust returns to dust, that the great random concatenation of chance and carbon and other stuff is ultimately barren, explicable and purposeless? Is it that our consciousness, that gift which is both boon and burden, cannot be satisfied by brutal fact, cannot accommodate our own mortality, cannot accept that what is, is and there's an end to it?

I'm afraid I do not know. The only thing I know for sure is why pigs appear always to be grinning.

Cheers for booze

Now is the season when family and friends come together in a spirit of festivity and get drunk. And what fun they have. Take a mob of malcontent dyspeptic uncles, frowzy aunts and mumbling grannies, drop a crate of Chateau Fizzy in their midst and watch the graph of pleasure soar.

The world abounds in lies. The three most famous are 'the cheque's in the mail', 'I love you' and another I can never remember. I can think of a plethora of candidates for that third spot – 'statistical proof' comes to mind, or any sentence containing the word 'honestly' – but the strongest and commonest of all the lies that encrust our mendacious little lives is that booze is a depressant. No matter how the medicos define depressant, I know depression and it does not come in bottles.

The same people as tell you this lie will tell you that tea is a stimulant. Have they never sat around a pot of tea and a plate of fancy cakes discussing knitting patterns with a bunch of women in tweed? No they haven't, and nor have I and I don't intend to. Any event that serves tea is funereal. If you want me I'll be in the pub.

Every human society has found a way of making booze. Only a few have tried to undo that knowledge. All have been fools and wrong. During Prohibition, for example, more drink tipped down American throats than ever tipped before or since. Those few countries where drink is illegal are the countries where hands are chopped off, feuds incessant and religion fanatical. And all the chiefs and bosses, sheikhs and sahibs knock it back a-plenty on the sly.

But, astonishingly, there's a deep and ugly streak of wowserism here in young New Zealand. No doubt it stems from fascinating historical causes which I want to know nothing about. It leaps to its feet when any liberal move is mooted. Women with clenched mouths, arched eyebrows and unthinkable frocks bemoan the moral decline. Bull-necked men with fat smug ties quiver at the jowls at the lowering of the drinking age, the dissolution of the church and the collapse of family values.

Most recently the legal drinking age came down from twenty to eighteen and oh the fuss of wowser-dom about it all. And do the youthful topers now run rampage through the night? And are our streets awash with howling teenage drunks? Of course they are. And so they were last year, and so the year before. But no, you're right, they weren't awash with teenage drunks in 1956 because the teenage drunks were hiding in the bush with woollen underwear and a stolen flagon of applejack. But that, of course, was kids being kids and having harmless fun.

26

And so it was. And so it is.

The wowsers call booze alcohol. They lie. If booze is alcohol then steak is nutrients and you and I are water. Booze is brandy, gin and wine; it's beer and rum and Amaretto, all rich and luscious words of ancient origin and faultless pedigree.

But the killjoys and the puritans will take me by the hand and lead me to the women's refuge and they will show me the suffering caused by drunks. And then they'll lead me to the morgue and show me drunken drivers smashed to bits and sober passengers with injuries that horrify.

Yes, yes, but then I will take them by the hand and lead them to the Lava Bar where men and women who have nothing in common but the freedom to be there, the money to spend there and too much to worry about are laughing. I will show them happy people. Or to the pub in Wellington we'll go and I will show them bureaucrats on Friday night whose ties have come undone and who no longer speak of target outcomes but are using nouns and verbs of simple honesty and whose jaws are sore from laughter. For every ounce of suffering I'll show a ton of lubricated joy.

Booze isn't respectable, of course. Anything that fosters honesty or pleasure is sure to be condemned in a society founded on repression. Booze lifts repression, dissolves inhibition and any psychologist will tell you over a glass of the best and finest what dreadful damage we do to ourselves with inhibitions. Drink is cheap psychotherapy. Drink opens the jailhouse door. It doesn't delude, it just

27

shortens the gap between thought and action. Drunks are more likely to say what they think and do what they want. And that is a very good thing. And despite the crashed cars and the damaged people and the stumblers with meths, as a general rule the gods look after drunks. Or at least they've looked after me. I can point at a wall in France which should have killed me. I can point at a donkey in the River Ebro and two cathedral roofs. I can point at memories that make me gurgle with delight. And so can thousands upon thousands.

Of course apologists for booze have tried to dress the stuff in Sunday best. They speak of responsible drinking as if the phrase were not by definition, praise the Lord, an oxymoron. And those who fangle metaphors for wine, who speak of crisp herbaceous noses, toasty finishes and hints of passionfruit are merely coining fancy words for fun. For yes, all wines taste different but not once you have got beyond the second sip. And now they've tried to do the same for beer. I know a newspaper that runs a column on beer. Oh spare us. Old Kingsley Amis, dead as mutton now, expressed it best, when he said all advertisements for beer could be reduced to one generic slogan: 'Drink Blank beer. It makes you pissed.'

Booze is a vast industry and an essential one. To ease our consciences we tax the stuff ferociously but still we pour it down. What staggers me is not how much damage booze wreaks, but how little, and in exchange it grants such easing of the mind, so much untrammelled laughter.

Dost thou think, because thou art virtuous, there shall be no more cakes and ale? Go sir, rub your chain with crumbs.

Happy New Year.

She smuggled a tortoise

'World,' wrote Louis MacNeice, 'is crazier and more of it than we think.' I have known these words for years and have indeed bored class after class of children with them. The children have yawned, I suspect, because to them the idea is obvious. But in middle age I find I lose sight of the truth of MacNeice's words. The world seems weary, stale, flat and unprofitable. But then something happens to remind me that it is sweetly crazy. This week, for example, I met a tortoise-smuggler.

The woman has smuggled only one tortoise, but that is one tortoise more than I have smuggled or am likely to smuggle.

Smuggler and tortoise met in Corfu, where the tortoise is apparently indigenous. This particular specimen, a small one, appeared by her bed one morning in the villa which she was renting. She took momentary fright, but the tortoise made no threatening move so she scooped it with a tray and bore it to the garden where she laid it gently down and watched it unfurl its neck and legs, nibble a snatch of something green for sustenance then head once more for the house. She raced it back and shut the door.

That evening the tortoise was at the step, whining silently to be let in. She left the door open. In the morning the tortoise was beside her bed. She let it stay, feeding it scraps of vegetable matter and sometimes a little pasta. It seemed contented and stayed for the remainder of her holiday. Once or twice she trod on it, but it did not take offence. She grew fond of it, she said.

I did not know that tortoises could show enough character to arouse affection. But this one had been, if nothing else, persistent and she said she liked its undemanding manner and also the curious way it drank.

At the end of the holiday she was loath to leave the tortoise. She did not flatter herself that the tortoise had attached itself specifically to her, but neither did she trust the next occupants of the villa to treat it with due kindness. She resolved to take it home to London with her.

She made enquiries of the authorities that deal with such things, and learned that it was illegal to import tortoises to Great Britain without a permit. Rabies was the problem. Now the woman in question is a responsible citizen. She insures her car and rarely drops litter and does not bury garden rubbish in her council bin bags. But when she weighed the issue she resolved that Great Britain had little to fear from a single tiny tortoise, even if it were later to foam at the mouth and go on rabid rampage.

So when she left she sat the tortoise in the bottom of her carry-on luggage along with an apple core and a carrot to keep it amused on the journey. As she passed through customs at Heathrow she felt the gaze of a dull-booted officer. She caught his eye, looked too swiftly away and was summoned. The officer rummaged unsmilingly through her suitcase, turning over her underwear and nightdresses and shaking a doll in native costume which she had bought for a niece. Then he indicated her shoulder bag. With tremulous fingers she emptied the contents on to his table, feeling no doubt as the frightfully rich American must have felt when the sniffer dog barked at his bag, although he, of course, was rightly let off on the grounds that if he had come to watch the America's Cup yachting then he needed every drug he could get.

The customs officer fingered her cosmetics, her tube of disposable contact lenses and then the tiny tortoise. It had, understandably, retracted its wrinkled head and feet. She said it was a brooch. The customs officer impounded the carrot and the apple core and let her go.

When she reached home she found the tortoise had eaten her lipstick and it was dead.

It is a little story and a sad one, but it filled me and thrilled me, in MacNeice's words, with 'the drunkenness of things being various'.

Pea neat

The gentle bumble bee, that harbinger of summer, visits a springtime blossom in much the same way as the Mongrel Mob visits a pensioner's house.

When a bee raids a sweet pea it perches on a small globe of petals just below the heart of the flower then buries its snout in nectar. The sweet pea appears to offer as much resistance to the theft as you would expect a sweet pea to offer, as much resistance indeed as most old people offer the Mongrel Mob.

But appearances deceive. When the bee lands it depresses the sweet pea's petals and causes them to separate. Through the slit between the petals a prong appears like a miniature rhino horn. The horn is tipped with yellow pollen as vivid as venom.

Just as when you visit the dentist you are so intent on what is going on in your mouth that you don't feel a thing as the wallet is removed from your back pocket, so the bee, intent on its nectar, doesn't notice as the pollen is smeared on its little furry buttocks. All unaware, it flies off to fertilize the next flower. It has become the winged inseminator. It is as if the elderly somehow managed to smear spermatozoa on the leather jackets of the Mongrel Mob, which is, I think, the point where that metaphor reaches the end of its useful life.

I discovered the cunning of the sweet pea during a traffic jam. Sweet peas proliferated in the lane in which I was jammed and I had nothing to do but study them. I was most impressed. The mechanism of the sweet pea seemed remarkably neat.

Such neatness in nature is just evolutionary ruthlessness. But neatness in people is folly. Neat people are prone to neurosis. I went to school with a boy who kept the same pencil case for seven years. His pencils were always sharpened. The coloured ones were held together with a rubber band and sorted for length. I guarantee that that boy now is either sad or mad. My money's on both.

For neat people seek to make life into a Fendalton drawing room, with floral wallpaper and all the furniture just so. But life isn't a Fendalton drawing room. It's more like an attic. The light doesn't work, you teeter on the floor joists, you can't find what you went there to fetch, you blunder into things you didn't go there to fetch, the things you didn't go there to fetch distract you and after a while you can't remember what you're doing there at all. Sometimes the roof permits you to stand to your full height and your spine unfurls with relief. You stride towards the future and headbutt a rafter.

Life's attic offers frustration, pain, puzzlement and occasional serendipitous delight. What it doesn't offer is neatness.

Don't expect neatness. The cosmos rarely does

neatness. Heaven does neatness because God made heaven, but down here in real time there's a neatness shortage because God doesn't (a) care, (b) exist.

But sometimes, just sometimes, you catch a glimpse of how things ought to be, a hint of the neat and the just, a glimmer of light in the dark, chaotic attic.

Take, for example, the traffic jam where I observed the bee and the pea. The lane was blocked by a removal van. Its cab was empty. Several other cars were already waiting.

The driver of the leading car got out. I recognized him as my local electrician, a man who will respond to an emergency call at the drop of a chequebook. He must, by now, have changed almost every bulb in my house. I joined him in the sunny lane with its sweet proliferation of peas and bees. The removal man, he said, was down below and he pointed at a little cottage where a benign and shaggy mongrel leapt cheerfully at a white gate.

The drivers in the traffic jam were mostly male and all frustrated. They sounded their horns like mastodons in rut. For a man in a car is a man with testosterone. At last he has the body God should have given him – 500 horsepower, a loud exhaust and a great big bonnet. He's king of the road, possums beware, hair in the wind and not to be messed with.

Behind their hot windscreens the stalled drivers fumed like bees in a jam jar. You could sense the hum of anger. They seethed with hatred for the removal man whose van blocked their rightful manly progress.

It was while I was studying the neatness of the sweet pea that Mr Inconsiderate emerged from the cottage. He sauntered into the sunlight as though the whole of time were his to spend. Horns greeted him. He looked up to see the line of traffic stretching back along the lane. To his credit he broke into a trot, reached the gate and bent to unlatch it. At this point the shaggy mongrel, boosted perhaps by the sun on its pelt and the unaccustomed activity, roused by the sight of a running removal man to memories of ancient hunts in distant lands, shook off the flimsy cloak of domesticity, reverted to the spirit of remote and feral wolves that roamed the winter wastes, and bit him on the buttock. The man yelped and we exulted.

It is unwise, I believe, to expect neatness, but there is no harm in rejoicing when it happens.

Dried pigs' ears

The girls were young and I was drunk. Not tumble-drunk but good drunk, benevolent drunk, the-world-is-an-all-right-place drunk. Drunk jolly, in other words, but not jolly drunk.

They were young and merry and sober. Two English girls, secretarial types, they were travelling in the manner made fashionable by young Australasians: go for a year or more, work a bit, live a bit, do it while you can. It is wholly admirable.

Seated at the bar the girls were lamps. Men were moths. One youth in particular blundered and pestered, got singed, flew straight back for more singeing, hauled to his doom by the blind imperative of pheromones. Quite why the girls started talking to me I don't know. Perhaps it was because in the dim light of bars I am sometimes mistaken for Paul Newman. Or perhaps it was to discourage the moths. Anyway, they did.

We talked of London and Melbourne. They told me some thin truths of their travels. I told them some good fat lies. We got on fine. They took me back years to when I did a little meek and solitary travelling of my own. And fired by beery benevolence and memories of the awkwardness of travel, the difficulties of washing and cooking, the awfulness of tents and rented beds, I said that they were welcome to come and stay at my house if they wished. They said thank you and goodbye and faded into the night air of Lyttelton, swatting as they went at the undissuadable moths. I went home singing in the rain until I reached the foot of the steep hill to my house. Then I just went home in the rain.

Sunday morning was Sunday morning. They are always much the same. Their indefinable Sunday-ishness squats on the shoulders like a dull monkey. Plutonium-grade coffee helped a bit and a long walk with the dogs a bit more and then I went to the shops for bread. As I pulled the car out of the drive the girls arrived. I pretended to be pleased, sent them up to the house to be mauled by the dogs. Driving down the road I cursed the generosity of beer. My solitude was broken. I had planned to work the Sunday, but I cannot work when people are in the house. I sense cramping eyes on my neck and the words go into hiding.

At the supermarket I bought a chicken on special. I would at least feed the girls well. I roast a fine chicken with garlic and rosemary and butter and, critically, lemon juice.

When I got back there was an orgy going on. The girls were murmuring baby talk and the treacherous dogs had rolled on to their backs to be tickled. The chicken beneath my arm, I felt like a caveman dragging a mammoth home to a family of ingrates.

The girls slept the afternoon. I tried to work but the Sundayishness of Sunday torpedoed me. I read and snoozed and at six I set to work on the bird. I buttered and garlicked and rosemaried it and found I'd forgotten to buy a lemon and thought to hell with it and flung it into the oven with oiled and salted potatoes. At six thirty the girls got up and were straight back down to dog stroking. Whimpers of delight all round. Even the cat sidled up for a piece of the action. At seven I boiled carrots. At seven ten I steamed asparagus into limpness. The girls remarked on the fine smells. At seven fifteen I served the chicken with a side salad of smugness. Both the girls were vegetarian. I ate the whole bird. It needed lemon juice. At eight the girls went out on a moth-hunt.

I went to bed early but for once I couldn't sleep. I got up and made a peanut butter sandwich. I turned the radio on and listened to a programme about religious chanting. But I found my mind running along old familiar tracks which I thought I had ripped up long ago. Round and round went the old debate of solitude against company, freedom against responsibility, selfishness against selfless- ness and the same old conclusions came and went like stations along the line.

Barking woke me. Barking turned to delighted whining. The girls were back. It was half past three. 'And where do you think you've been? Well? What have you got to say for yourselves? I've been worried sick, I have,' I muttered to the pillow and went straight back to sleep. When I woke again they had gone for good. There was a bottle of wine on the table and a pair of dried pigs' ears, one for each dog. The dogs will miss the girls.

Of chopping and sticking

It was not a successful evening. For a start I went grudgingly, because – well, you don't need the details. Let me just say that I went to say sorry. I had been in the wrong, of course, but that was all water under the bridge, or at least last night was meant to shove the water under the bridge and out into the great ocean of forgiveness. I planned, in short, to eat humble pie.

But I didn't eat humble pie. I ate Chinese. Chinese food does little for me. I have yet to find flavour in either noodles or rice. And then, of course, I got chopsticks.

Well now, I am as dextrous as the next man. But I do not hold with chopsticks. Chopsticks are sticks. Sticks are bad cutlery.

Chopsticks do not chop and neither do they stick. If they were pointed you could at least spear the more substantial bits, but they aren't so you can't. And if a competition were held to discover the food least suited to consumption by chopsticks, rice would get the silver medal and noodles the gold.

We are supposed to be a tool-making species. Tool making is what has raised us into dominion over the beasts of the field and the birds of the air and the fishes of the sea. And when it comes to eating the beasts, birds and fishes, and in particular the smaller vegetables, the fork is a better tool than chopsticks. The spoon is a better tool than chopsticks. Indeed, virtually everything in your pockets is a better tool than chopsticks.

I do not mind other people using chopsticks. Though it may seem to me that those who are adept with chopsticks still use them mainly as shovels, and I find it impossible to imagine a worse design for a shovel, nevertheless, as I say, I have no quarrel with the users of chopsticks. Let them depart in peace.

Those I do have a quarrel with are those who expect me to use chopsticks. And these people are never those who were brought up with the things. Chinese restaurateurs are always delighted to fetch me my preferred weaponry.

No, the people who think it somehow right to use chopsticks to eat a dish that has been cut into little bits and laid on a bed of even littler bits, are people who were raised as I was raised with a silver-plated fork in the mouth. But when I call for a fork they look at each other in a mixture of shock and disdain and they tut. They consider me an oaf.

Now I do not deny oafdom. Oaf is a speciality of the house. But I fail to see why it should be considered a further black mark on my much marked escutcheon for me to wish to eat my food efficiently. It seems unreasonable. But reason, of course, doesn't come into it.

What does come into it is sycophancy, the belief that somehow one will ingratiate oneself with people from overseas by doing as they do. Wrong, of course. Restaurateurs of any breed don't give a fig how you eat their food. They give a fig only about whether you pay for it.

But the sycophants go further. By using chopsticks, they believe, one is leaving one's comfort zone and getting the authentic cultural experience.

Well phooey to that. For a start I like my comfort zone. I find it comfortable. But more significantly, I can think of no phrase more barren of meaning than authentic cultural experience. Authentic cultural experience means Disneyland. Authentic cultural experience means watching dances by grass-skirted people who, if you weren't paying them, would be wearing jeans and not dancing. Authentic cultural experience means bogus, artificial boredom.

All of which, of course, I didn't say. I was supposed to be behaving so I just bit my lip, grabbed a chopstick in each hand and spent a bitter evening scattering food. Hungry and angry make potent bedfellows. The water remains this side of the bridge and seems to have increased in volume.

The stars above

'It is the stars, the stars above us, govern our conditions,' said the Earl of Kent in Act IV of *King Lear*.

The great Earl comes to mind today because I have just had lunch with the Wise Woman. The Wise Woman, you must understand, is not the sort of hut-dwelling wise woman with a hooked nose, a black cat and a cupboardful of dried dog's-tongue, but a modern wise woman with a degree in something I don't understand and a PhD in something I seriously don't understand. She and I get on famously by disagreeing about everything. Our lunches resemble the Battle of the Somme.

Today, over a flat white sandwich and a long black coffee we amiably scratched at each other's eyes for a while then discussed why it is that we always disagree. Then Wise Woman asked me my star sign.

Across the rubble of plates, coffee cups and spent verbal bullets, I told her I was a Virgo. And that, it seemed, explained everything. Wise Woman told me that she always fought with Virgos. Virgos were, she said, dogmatic, sullen, intransigent, cantankerous, rebarbative – and a thesaurus-load of other adjectives, few of which I can remember but all of which combined to mean that she and a Virgo could simply never rub along.

I chewed over the abuse and my flat white sandwich. I sipped at my coffee and her long black words. For I had to admit that she had caught my character like a fly in amber. She had me sprawling on her pin. Perhaps because we were lunching in public and every wall sprouted ears, she had omitted some of my juicier failings, nevertheless she had said more than enough and every syllable of the reckoning was bang on and damning. Except for one teensy-weensy point. I am not a Virgo.

The Wise Woman is not the first of her kind to biff me with the Zodiac. In the last decade, 3281 women have asked me my star sign. In the same period the number of men who have done so is roughly 0.

I think I sniff a gender issue. I have always wanted a gender issue. Lots of people seem only to have to turn over the rock of any public matter to find a gender issue crawling underneath, but I have never found one before and I am excited. I have also recently lacked hate-mail.

Why is it, then, that so many women and so few men take an interest in the Zodiac, that sensible, talented women subscribe to the idea that lumps of cooling matter a squillion or so light years away affect our natures at birth? Why do they not recognize the self-evident truth that it is so much hocus-pocus?

For it is hocus-pocus, the most obvious drivel, the sort of spritual driftwood that we feel the urge to cling to as we toss on the faithless seas of twentieth-century rationalism. Why can so many women not accept that all this business about Saturn in the ascendant makes as much sense as a Treasury forecast?

Furthermore, why can they not see that so many of the definitions of character in the astrologists' rantings are paradoxical? I, for example, am actually a Scorpio. (Don't tell me; you guessed as much. Well, you were right. Well done.) But at different times I have been told that Scorpios are extroverts and I have been told that they are shy. I have been told that Scorpios are secretive and that they are candid.

'Do I contradict myself?' asked Walt Whitman. 'Very well then,' continued old Walt, 'I contradict myself. I am large, I embrace multitudes.'

And that is exactly the point. We all embrace multitudes. We all know ourselves to be both heroes and cowards. We know ourselves to be both generous and selfish, wise and foolish, rash and cautious. Astrologers know it too and rely on it.

But how come so many women subscribe to it? Women, of course, are much nicer than men. They take an interest in other people while men take endless interest only in themselves.

Robert Graves began 'A Slice of Wedding Cake' with the following question:

Why have such scores of lovely, gifted girls
Married impossible men?

46

Graves couldn't answer the question, and neither can I. But nor can I tell you why so many women seem to believe there are only twelve types of people. Is it, as the Wise Woman suggested, that women seek a system of belief that is not dominated by men? It might be so. Answers on a postcard, please, to my spiritual home c/o Aries the ram. (Yes, of course, you knew all along. Same birthday as Hitler, as it happens.)

Aleppo

I used to teach him English. Now he's teaching me geography. In the traditional manner of the young he's gone travelling, having first bought one of those compulsory little money belt pouch things that keep passport and traveller's cheques conveniently close to the genitals so that everything can be defended at once when abroad turns nasty.

He's just sent me an e-mail from Aleppo. If, yesterday, you had stopped me in the street and asked me where Aleppo was, I would have been surprised, but I would have said Egypt. And I would have been wrong. I now know it's in Syria, although, to be frank, that doesn't help much. It invites an obvious second question, which is where Syria is. I think it may be in Egypt.

Everything else that I know of Aleppo I got from Shakespeare.

Early in *Macbeth* the first witch tells the story of a woman who is roasting chestnuts. The witch describes the woman as a rump-fed ronyon – and who hasn't met a few of those? Lyttelton seethes with them – but anyway the witch asks her for some chestnuts. The ronyon replies 'aroint, thee witch' which translates loosely as 'no'. It is not a wise reply.

The witch happens to know that the ronyon's husband is a mariner. He has recently sailed for Aleppo. The witch resolves to follow him – travelling rather ostentatiously by sieve. She promises that once she gets to Aleppo, 'I'll do, I'll do, and I'll do.'

What she'll do she doesn't specify but you sense that the ronyon may soon be selling chestnuts full time to supplement her widow's pension.

Anyway, my former pupil with the money belt pouch thing is in Aleppo and by all accounts he's having a wizard time. But then having a wizard time is what you do when travelling. Few people send postcards moaning that they are bored, lonely or frightened. Travel's good and brave and exhilarating. Travel means striding manfully towards the heroic horizon with one's money belt pouch thing swinging audaciously in the warm winds of hope.

And of course I envy the lad. How could one not envy him Aleppo? When you drop it into a conversation, Aleppo lands with so much more of a clang than, say, Ashburton.

Aleppo's such a squalid-romantic name. It sings of tall donkey-coloured buildings with a smallpox of bullet holes, narrow streets, fetid beggars, men with stumps, women with washing, flies, dogs, danger and all the other tourist attractions.

Time was when I'd have hauled my money belt pouch thing from the dusty cupboard and hi-hoed for Aleppo at the drop of an e-mail. In those days the horrible walls of habit hadn't grown so high that I couldn't peep over them and take a peek at all the other lovely places. Atlases made me salivate. Travel ads trembled my knees. What they depicted was Elsewhere, that glorious place where I wasn't. And off I would trot.

I didn't trot well. I made nothing happen. If things did happen it was because someone else made them happen, some quaint local with unquaint idiosyncrasies. He or she would do something unpredictable involving knives or drugs or budgerigars and I would find myself in a hole I didn't think I could clamber out of. I always did clamber out, of course, but even as I did so I would be mentally rehearsing the story I could tell when I got home. I still tell those stories. They're crackers. They make me laugh. They didn't make me laugh at the time.

But the real trouble was that whenever I got to the place I was trotting to I found it was no longer Elsewhere. I'd imported something to spoil it and that something was me. In direct consequence I spent most of my time being scared or bored or lonely or the whole trifecta and pining for the tall walls of habit.

I think it was a character in a Hardy poem who said that you can see everything there is to see from your own back doorstep. I know it was a character in a Graves poem who said that every ocean smells alike of tar. And I know now that to the citizens of Aleppo, paradise is Ashburton. Elsewhere is a universal myth.

Elsewhere is of a piece with yesterday and tomorrow. You never get there. It's one of the roast chestnuts that the rump-fed ronyon of life tempts you with but never hands over. So why is it that even now, the thought of the strangeness of Aleppo makes something in my stomach deliquesce? I think it may be just the sound of the place. Aleppo.

Small stuff

There's a book called *Don't Sweat the Small Stuff*. I haven't read it because it's a self-improvement book and no self-improvement book has ever improved anyone except the author whom it often improves to the tune of several zillion bucks. But the title of this book intrigues me.

If, as I imagine, it advises the reader not to get swamped by trivia, but rather to keep his entrepreneurial eye forever trained on the horizon of opportunity where the big stuff roams, then I think it's hogwash. Big stuff sounds good but means little. 'Life,' said somebody, 'is just one damned thing after another'. Truth, such as it is, lies in the small stuff. It is always with us. The stuff like letter boxes.

When I bought my house it came with a letter box. It was a wooden letter box and a frail one but it did the job. It safely held the fizzing hate-mail and the accusations of dud grammar. It held the cheques I receive for writing stuff, and it even held a magnifying glass to read them with. The only thing my little letter box wouldn't hold on to was love letters. They dissolved like edible underwear.

Perhaps they were written on edible underwear. Or perhaps the jealous dogs got to them first. But otherwise the letter box was sound.

Then one night its little roof blew off. I set to work repairing it with some fine wire nails and a dainty cabinet-maker's hammer, and in no time at all I had returned it to what it started as – which was several pieces of wood. They made good kindling.

Warm but letter boxless I took a catering-sized jam bucket and nailed it horizontally to a post.

Back indoors I wrote 'letter box' in my 'Things to do' book. The 'things to do' book is my way of handling the small stuff. When there's something I've got to do I write it in the book. When I've done it, I cross it out.

The aim of my life is to cross out all the small stuff. Then I can put my feet on the windowsill and gawp at the big stuff as God intended. But I never cross everything out. In fact my 'things to do' book reads like an inverse autobiography. My successes have all been crossed out but my failures stand tall. They're as persistent and shaming as genital warts. The letter box is one such.

Every day for two years my letter box has reproached me. 'You are idle,' it mutters, 'I am a jam bucket. Get a letter box. Everyone else has got a letter box.'

And because I've got a bad letter box, I notice that everyone else has got a good one. Fired by envy, I have become a connoisseur of letter boxes. I have noticed, for example, that three models dominate the suburban letter-box market – The Grim, The Gruesome and The Twee.

The Grim is the Stalinist letter box. It is built of thin sheet metal painted anonymous cream. It's square as a shoebox, and smooth as a Martian's skull. It has a slot in its forehead and nothing else.

The Gruesome purports to be decorative and is normally to be found amid psychotically neat borders of flowering annuals. It consists of a metal stake sunk into the ground, a crossbar extending from the top of the stake and the kite-shaped letter box dangling from it like a corpse on a gallows.

The most popular design is the Twee. The Twee is wooden and looks like a miniature Swiss chalet. Under its steeply pitched eaves there's a triangular slot for newspapers, beneath that a compartment for letters with a flap at the back and beside that a compartment to house the lovely, bulky, promising parcels I never get.

And yesterday I bought a Twee. I wasn't looking for it. I chanced upon it outside one of those second-hand shops that sells dirty pieces of sadness. The price was right and the Twee was mine.

Back home I dug a hole and sank half a railway sleeper into it. I packed the earth around and trod it down. The thing stood firm. I placed the Twee on top of it and nailed it into place. I didn't hit my thumb and the Twee didn't split. I put lots of nails in. I shook it. It stood as solid as the Treasury. I tore the jam bucket from its mooring and threw it away.

Every five minutes I returned to check my letter box. Its firmness thrilled me. Its neatness delighted me. I kept opening and closing the flap for the joy that was in it. The postie arrived. She handed me a bill. I asked her to put it in the slot. She put it in the slot. I opened the flap and there was the bill. It was a fine moment. It was good small stuff. In my 'things to do' book I crossed out 'letter box' and wrote 'pay bill'.

A good old story

Good stories are common as sparrows. But stories of good are less common, and stories of good which are also good stories are as rare as the kakapo. But such a story has just hatched. It is the story of Mr Cronje. In case you missed the news, Mr Cronje was captain of the South African cricket team, an outfit renowned for its frivolity. Mr Cronje added his bit to the fun by having a face carved from the sort of concrete that makes the Christchurch Town Hall such a pretty building. He also wore the permanently blue chin of a man whose masculinity is not to be doubted.

Mr Cronje was renowned for playing hard but fair. Hard but fair is normally a euphemism meaning nasty and keen to cheat. But in Mr Cronje's case it seemed to mean what it says. Under his leadership the South African cricket team has spent the last few years trampling on the tracheas of their opponents and thereby bringing great joy to themselves and to a lot of South Africans. Mr Cronje expressed his joy by scowling, thus giving further joy. He and his team seemed not to know self-doubt and so thrashed teams like England who justifiably ooze it. Sports teams who believe that sport matters and who believe that they are going to win, win. The meek do not inherit the world cup.

But, as we all know, Mr Cronje no longer captains South Africa. He tossed away a jewel worth more than his tribe. He sold his soul for a mess of pottage, in the form of a few thousand dollars from an Indian bookmaker. The police got wind of the deal and whispered a word or two, it seems, to the South African Cricket Board who in turn whispered some questions to Mr Cronje.

Mr Cronje denied wrongdoing. He denied it with vigour. He denied it repeatedly. His denials were blazoned across headlines across the world. And although people love to see the prominent tumble, and although people tend to believe that there is no smoke without a bloody great bonfire somewhere, I suspect that most people doubted that Mr Cronje had done anything wrong, because although Mr Cronje seemed a dull man, he seemed also to be an incorruptible man. It was unthinkable that he should have done anything so venal and foolish.

Well, the unthinkable should always be thought. Scepticism, especially in matters of power and money – which are synonyms – is a virtue. And so, of course, it transpired. Mr Cronje had indeed done it. He had taken the moolah. Why he took it in one sense remains a mystery, for he was prospering and the sum given was comparatively trivial, but he took it. In the end I suspect he was just greedy. You and I are of course immune to greed, but Mr Cronje, it seems, is not. Let's have fun casting stones at him.

But the greed is less interesting than the way the story unfolded. From what I can gather, Mr Cronje got walloped by the middle-of-the-night blues. For it seems that after a day of denials and of being followed by photographers and other crustacea, none of whom had the least apparent effect on him, Mr Cronje went home and went to bed.

And bed got him. What the press could not do and what Mr Ali Bacher of the South African Cricket Board could not do, bed did. For Mr Cronje was not in bed alone. He lay wide-eyed and sleepless with a small voice. The voice urged him to own up.

He was faced with the dilemma which faced Macbeth. Should he ignore the voice and harden his heart and plough deeper into the trough of amoral success or should he come clean and purge the bosom of that perilous stuff which weighed upon the heart? Macbeth chose the former. Mr Cronje, bless him, chose the latter.

At three in the morning he rose from his bed and he rose as a man and he telephoned Mr Bacher and pronounced himself guilty. How did he feel when he did so? He felt cleansed. By admitting his weakness he became strong. He knew as he owned up that he could face every stone that you or I could cast at him. He could stand before the baying mob in the impenetrable armour of honesty. He had hurt himself. We could no longer hurt him.

Mr Cronje is apparently a devout Christian but I don't believe that matters.

For Christianity, like all religions, merely

acknowledges the human condition and supplies a framework of words and metaphors to accommodate it. Christianity did not invent good or evil or conscience or honesty or confession. These things are as old as people. And to see them work out again and again in human affairs, always the same, always the old old story, revives one's faith in a sorry world, reminds us that there is no guilt so great that it cannot be confessed, nor any crime so wicked that it cannot be forgiven, and confirms that, beneath the tat and triumphal emptiness of a society mad for sport and washing machines, certain truths hold true as stone.

Rite rite

They must exist the whole year round, I suppose, but I hear of them only occasionally. One of those occasions was last week when they popped their heads above the parapets once more and squeaked their dangerous nonsense.

They are the Simplified Spelling Society – or, presumably, the Simplifide Speling Sosiyutee. The Simplies have been around for a long time and have never got very far, but I don't see that as any reason to stop me sticking the boot into their ideas.

I have never met a Simplie but I imagine them to be bearded people in sweaters the colour of vinegar. No doubt they're not. No doubt they're all clean-shaven and decorated in nice bright acrylic sweaters from Deka, and no doubt they breed lovely children and give generously to charity, but my image of them is born of my distaste for their ideas. They would like to fiddle with the English language. I would like to cut their fiddling fingers off.

Although the English language has provided me with a living of sorts for a couple of decades, I have yet only the scantiest knowledge of its complexities. English is like a coral reef. It has grown over the centuries by a process of slow accretion and slower erosion. It has fed on everything that has floated past it and absorbed what it has found useful. Though the fat dictionaries may suggest the language is a fixed and lumpish thing, it is alive and in constant change.

It is also resilient. It allows all manner of politicians, sports commentators and guidance counsellors to torture it, and yet it retains a sinuous strength that rebounds undamaged from all assaults.

Because the roots of English lie partly in Anglo-Saxon and partly in Latin and partly in French, and because English has accommodated offerings from a host of other tongues, and because it has been put to use in a mass of different climates and circumstances, and because it has always welcomed change, English has become a difficult language to spell. Through does not rhyme with though, nor with cough or bough or enough or thorough. I find that delightful. The Simplies don't. If they had their way these words would become something like thru, tho, coff, bow, enuf and thura.

And no doubt the Simplies would argue that they would thus make the language easier to read and write. Their argument would certainly find favour with such august institutions as the Ministry of Education and the New Zealand Qualifications Authority who have applied the same principle to exams: if children can't pass them then the obvious solution is to make the exams easier.

The educational mandarins are proved wrong

every day and the Simplies are similarly wrong. Even if spelling were utterly logical and consistent, just as many children would spell badly. Maths, for example, is logical and consistent yet plenty of children fail to grasp it.

I have taught several thousand children. Some could spell and some couldn't and most lay in between. By and large those who could spell were readers and those who couldn't weren't. I also taught plenty of children who had been told they were dyslexic and not a few who actually were. But I found that, with hard work, even the most severe dyslexics could gain some mastery over their problems. They could even learn to spell dyslexia. They certainly had a harder road to ride than people like me who find it easy to spell almost everything except inoculate and gauge, but I do not believe that the language should be altered to suit people who find spelling hard. It would be like taking the high jump out of the Olympics because some people have short legs.

Most words carry their history with them. Their roots can be found in the spelling. Change the spelling and those roots would be harder to trace. Though language moves on and meanings alter, and etymology rarely grants us the present meaning of a word, nevertheless when the winds of stupidity blow roots can act as an anchor.

But not only would the simplification of spelling distance the language from its roots, more importantly still it would sever the people of tomorrow from the wisdom of yesterday. A reasonably educated speaker of English can read Chaucer in the original. Mess about with the spelling and Chaucer would become as impenetrable as Sanskrit. So would Shakespeare, Dickens, Bacon, Eggers and *Goodbye Mr Chips*.

Lose your past and you lose everything. All the thinking has to be done over again. The language brings with it the gains and the wisdom of yesterday.

The first act of the totalitarian leaders of 1984 was to modernize the language and thus to cripple independent thought and the gains of history. All unwitting, the Simplies wish to commit a similar Orwellian atrocity on our tongue. No doubt they mean well but they would encourage the descent of the Dark Ages. Theirs is an innocent arrogance.

Yurt and yak

Why do we surround ourselves with stuff? Now is the season of stuff, of course, almost all of it dreadful stuff, combination-barbecue-tool type stuff, or matching-nail-clipper-and-shampoo-set stuff, the sort of stuff that will be garage sale fodder within months. A few more months and it will go permanently to ground where it will leach nasties to poison our progeny for the next few millennia, but no one cares much about that for obvious reasons. And anyway that's not the sort of stuff I mean.

The sort of stuff I mean is the art stuff. By art stuff I mean the pretty stuff, the expressive stuff, the stuff we display on walls or shelves to make our homes, well, nicer.

The ancient nomads didn't go in for art stuff. They loaded the yak with the yurt and the saucepans but they biffed the Titian on the fire because it served no purpose. But as soon as nomads settled down, as soon as they found themselves a cave in one of the nicer suburbs, they started painting reindeer on the walls. They became civilized, which etymologically means nothing more than that they lived in towns. With civilization came the art stuff. And it came to stay. We modern hunter-gatherers have ditched the yak and the yurt, and we go hunting only in supermarkets, but we've underlined the gathering. We call it collecting. I wonder if we're wise.

The people who gave me lunch and bubbly yesterday collect a species of crockery called Carltonware. It's chunky fifties stuff painted a distinctive bile green. The details are picked out in lung-pink and vomit-yellow. They've got cabinets crammed with the stuff. Whenever I visit them I stare at the stuff as I would at a butcher's window.

These people also collect paintings. Barely an inch of their walls is bare. They have lived in the same house for thirty years and their collection of art stuff has grown around them like a coral reef. They do not mean to move. The prospect of shifting all that stuff from the walls to the back of a yak would daunt the toughest nomad. Easier and wiser to stay and gather.

I don't go in for visual art stuff, though I did once buy a painting of a cabbage at the opening of an exhibition where champagne abounded. I have the painting still and hate it.

But I do go in for books. I love to own books. Though I read few books twice, I have filled every shelf in my house with books, have had more shelves made and have filled those too. My books surround me like a cocoon. When I run my finger along the backs of my books they feel like the ribcage of an old familiar lover. Visit my shelves and you will learn much about me.

And that, perhaps, is the nub of the matter. The art stuff we put on our walls and our shelves, the stuff we cram into display cabinets, anything from cats in brandy balloons to the works of Dostoevsky, announces something about us. We paste our tastes and tendencies upon our walls to produce a cradle of self in which to live. It is both a vanity and a reassurance, a bulwark against a world that cares too little about us.

But what will happen when I go to the eternal landfill? Someone presumably will go through my books, keeping a few perhaps but selling off the bulk of them too cheaply to someone who trades in the unwanted chattels of the dead. My collection will disintegrate like the atoms of my flesh. My books will scatter to second-hand bookshops where people like myself will pick them over, buying the pieces that suit their image of themselves and will shelve them, to build up their own collection, their own vain expression of self, like a stork selecting twigs to build a nest.

Perhaps the nomads were right. A yurt and a yak and a wide wide sky.

Emotion in aspic

When your grandmother died did you go through her things, the remnants of a lived life, and find, tucked away under some linen perhaps, or clasped within the covers of a book, a little bundle of letters tied with pink ribbon? Did you then gently untie that frayed and faded ribbon, feeling like a trespasser as you did so, slide a letter from an envelope, flatten the creases in the paper that time had made frail, and read in faded ink the ancient words of love? No, nor did I.

But I would have liked to do so. For I relish letters. Letters are gifts. More honest than photographs, letters are emotion in aspic. Letters are as personal as touch. They can be held, treasured, folded in pockets and purses, sniffed and kissed, or torn in two and burned.

Other people's letters are a voyeur's delight. Published collections of the letters of eminent people sell well, because they are the best form of autobiography. Good letters sing with honesty. In letters you do not find the evasions, omissions and half-truths that make autobiographies into works of fiction. No one polishes a letter for posterity, except, that is, W. B. Yeats who sometimes asked for his letters back so that he could amend them.

Of the letters I have received over the years only one has changed my life. But of the thousands of others, many have given joy.

What pleases so about letters is that they are links to a past, like the streamers thrown to shore when a liner leaves port. But now, I fear, the letter is threatened. E-mail is taking over. E-mail is a priceless business tool, but it lacks romance. It has the permanence and elegance of a hamburger.

Because e-mail is so easy, swift and cheap, people use it too much. Most e-mail messages are blurts, ill-spelt, ill-chosen and ill-considered spasms of words, as significant as sneezes. While a good letter is a butterfly, netted and gassed some distant summer and now pinned forever under glass, an e-mail is a blowfly, common, black, ugly, dirty and dead.

But in a world without butterflies a man must clutch at blowflies. Today I received an e-mail from Ben who is exiled in Belgium. Living in Belgium is doing it tough. Belgium is all cream and hideous dolls in national dress and bourgeoisie and smothering boredom relieved only by a horrific subculture of fat pederasts. Ben has not lived abroad before and is homesick. He has been torn up by the roots. He is pining for Ashburton. It's that serious.

He tells me that a day without e-mail from down under is a dire day, that he needs a fix of contact with his past to buoy him through his present. E-mail is his lifeline.

His words took me back. When I left university some time around the end of the nineteenth century I somehow fetched up in Spain and love.

I soon fell out of love but stayed in Spain. I was not homesick but, surrounded by a foreignness of which I was no part, I felt the need for contact from my elsewhere. E-mail was not yet a glint in Bill Gates' eye. I longed for airmail letters whose blue and red edging is the sexiest colour I know. An empty letter box stung.

With springwater clarity I remember one afternoon when I went back to a flat on the thirteenth floor in Calle de Felisa Gale, a flat from which I had been kicked out after a spat over domestic chores. Calle de Felisa Gale lay on the far side of the city but a couple of months after leaving I walked the five miles back there in the hope of letters. I found a dozen fat airmail envelopes awaiting me. It was like stumbling on the end of the rainbow. On the return trek across the city, I read as I walked. Engrossed in words, I crossed Avenida Generalissimo Mola and was hit a sidelong blow by a yellow Fiat. It spun me out of the past and into the gutter of now. But I cherish letters still.

And the letter that changed my life? I can quote it in full. I had written in mawkish self-pity to a friend in Paris. The reply, 'Know what you are and be it, creep.'

Seduced

I've been seduced again, thank God. My seducer was E. B. White the essayist, Elwyn perhaps to his wife and family, but E.B. to those of us who read him. And old E.B. of whom I have never seen a photograph but whom I imagine wearing old-man tweeds and wise-man glasses, seduced me by telling me of his chickens. He wrote of Golden Wyandottes and Speckled Orpingtons and I was sold.

I have been seduced by chickens before. Thirty years ago my brother bought two battery hens at an auction. They wore a few anaemic feathers, and their legs wobbled. He took the sad birds home, fed them grain and grass and freedom and within weeks they stood proud and brown, birds to daunt a dog, strutting fowl with combs as dramatic as lipstick on a courtesan.

Fired by the memory and by old E.B. I resolved to start the century with chickens. From there I might move on to pigs, geese and a goat. From a woman of the soil I borrowed *Self Sufficiency*, a book that spoke in entertaining terms of how to rear a pig, feed it skimmed milk, nurse it through the illnesses of piglethood and kill it. And then, having killed it, how to saw around its anus, hack its innards out and hang its hocks and hams amid the chimney-piece to smoke their way to bacon. I crossed pig off my list. I have a gas fire.

At the same time I had also to acknowledge that I am no farmer. I am as rural as Woody Allen. Because my hands are pudgy-white and I am nervous of cattle I would be unwise to plunge into animal husbandry. I should enter into it with caution as into a hard-hat area – although I do sometimes wonder whether anyone in the history of hard hat areas has ever known a brick to land on his hard hat – and my means of entry, my introduction to the self-sufficient life, would be chooks. Their needs, I read, are few.

Having surfed the internet for chicken-house designs, I emerged from under my house with a hammer, a box of ancient nails and enough discarded timber to build an ark and as I lugged it all up the garden I strove to remember what I had learned in woodwork classes thirty years ago. I recalled my nonagenarian teacher telling me not to waste wood because it didn't grow on trees, and I recalled triumphantly carrying home my first successful project and being hugely praised for it – so well-made was that chopping board that I believe my mother still uses it – but otherwise I recalled nothing.

Five minutes into henhouse construction it all came back. What came back was the joy of swinging the hammer squarely on to a thumbnail. The only sensation I know to match it is stubbing a toe. In both instances the pain lurks offstage for perhaps two seconds. That seems the worst moment because you know with terrified bewilderment that the pain will come. But it is not the worst moment. The worst moment is when the pain comes. It surges with a ferocity that makes you yearn for amputation. I clenched the thumb between my thighs, then held it as far away from me as possible, then ran around the garden shouting. The dogs joined in the game.

But I persevered and slowly a chookhouse grew. It held perches and nest boxes and sliding doors that sometimes slid, and a ramp leading into a pen of straw and other pens of grass – the Balfour system which I had read about. Above the pen stands a plum tree which in autumn will bombard the chickens with their lunch. And all was dog-proof too, as I confirmed by placing a bone in the middle of it.

One day later, closely attended by a brace of dogs and studied from afar by a cat, I eased the lid off a banana box and released three hens, the offspring of a Rhode Island Red and something equally traditional, into the surprise of a new world. Within minutes they were scratching through the straw for grain. Within hours they had eaten the grass. Within a day they had strutted, clucked and pecked their way into my heart. I lack the space here to say how. Perhaps I also lack the words to convey the deep contentment of a chicken's brooping, or the iridescence of the black-green feathers on its back or the spearing accuracy of its beak guided by a round primeval eye.

This week I got my first egg, laid as neat and clean as any supermarket egg on a hollow of straw. It was warm. I fried it in butter. It was a fine egg. It cost me $35 for chicken wire, $9.95 for tin-snips to cut the wire, $8 to replace the scissors that failed to cut the wire, $6 for a bag of wheat, $12 for layer pellets, $7 for straw, $20 for the hens themselves, ten minutes a day for tending to their needs and two hours a day for leaning on the fence to admire them. And I got, I reckon, a bargain.

Moving bad things

Bad things don't go away. You can put them in a cupboard but when you move house the bad things will still be in the cupboard. And they will have got worse.

So it was that Tom and Cathy – they asked me not to use their real names which are Patrick and Jeanette – discovered that they owned six tangerine-coloured Indonesian floating candles, a roll of slug tape, floral placemats, a teapot with a wicker handle, ancient secateurs and a dead microwave as big as a tomb. Tom and Cathy knew exactly what to do with stuff that no one could possibly want. They held a garage sale.

By inviting friends to contribute items they amassed a cornucopia of tat. I warned Cathy that I knew of a man who held a garage sale and had most of the best items stolen. She appointed me official security guard.

The sale began at 8.30 so I arrived promptly to guard it at 10. The house was humming. Tom was sizzling sausages, and cutting up onions. Everyone else was cutting deals. Well-dressed women were leaving with armfuls of *Home and Garden* magazines from the mid-nineties. The teapot with the wicker handle had gone. Students had snapped up the orange armchairs. Those chairs will now be sitting on a verandah getting wet and leaking stuffing. The students also took the microwave.

Stock was running low so despite my security role I was put to work. I carried out from the house a spice rack with two jars, a soap dish shaped like a fish, a leather Jim Beam bottle-holder, a wire fruit bowl, black women's shoes 'worn only once' – presumably because the wearer broke her ankle – a floral lampshade, an iron with stains, two rolls of dissimilar wallpaper, a set of earphones with cobwebs and torn padding, a hardened paint roller, a mug-tree, a golf trolley without wheels or handle and a watercolour print of flowers which I dropped for aesthetic reasons. The glass shattered. I put the shards on a table, then sat on a wall to eat sausages and catch thieves.

The goods were not good. Yet somehow, somewhere, someone had thought they needed to be invented, manufactured and distributed to the waiting world. Now, after a life of neglect, they sat in a suburban driveway, like orphans begging for a home. Little of the stuff was useful, and none of it beautiful. But it sold.

For four hours the driveway was rarely empty. People of all descriptions came and went. Second-hand dealers swooped, assessing the tat, snatching a piece of it, halving the price, moving on, collecting a trailerful. They must have been up at dawn to plan the best route round the city of classified ads.

75

Whole families came, with girls in ponytails and boys in cargo pants. Men came on bicycles and didn't take off their helmets. Studious people turned the china over to check the maker's stamp. A local celebrity bought the paint roller for fifty cents, and discussed classical music over a sausage.

Commerce dwells in our blood. Few people bought things because they needed them. They bought them because they were cheap. Despite a voice in my head I found I couldn't resist a bottle of aftershave I wouldn't use, a briefcase I didn't need and the ancient secateurs.

The students came back. The microwave had spat arcs of blue plasma at them. They spent their refund on a mirror and the Jim Beam stand.

Time and again the tables emptied and the sellers, drunk with the joy of trading, scurried to their houses to retrieve more detritus. Digging out stuff turned out to be like vomiting: there was always a little more to come. Unused council rubbish bags marked 'not to be sold' sold instantly. Someone bought a Thai Airlines promotional handbag.

The floating candles had been a gift – presumably from the blind to the unloved. Tom asked the mature woman who bought them whether she was planning a romantic evening. She snorted. A woman in pink bought the statue which I have been asked to describe as African in case the relatives who brought it back from South America read this. She paid $4.

A man picked up the largest shard of glass from the picture I had broken. He turned it over, studied it and for one thrilling moment I thought he was going to make an offer. But he bought the slug tape instead.

It was a happy gentle morning. In four hours over 600 untaxed black-market dollars changed hands, almost all of it in coins. Hundreds of ugly things moved home. The last rites were delivered by a chap from a church who ate two cooling sausages and took away everything unsold for nothing.

When I got home I snipped at the hedge with my secateurs. They broke. I put the aftershave in the briefcase, and the briefcase in a cupboard.

Of doers and doodlers

I know four bits of German. The first three of them, in what seems to me to be the right order, are tank, leather trousers and eleven beers please. I learned them on a cricket tour of the British Army of the Rhine.

My fourth bit of German is the useful word Zeitgeist. It means literally the ghost of the time, less literally the spirit of the age. But though I like the word Zeitgeist, I do not like its present manifestation. For I am out of tune with the Zeitgeist.

The Zeitgeist requires us to be driven people. Efficiency is today's watchword. We are to be busy and keen, urged on by achievement, lured by the dangling carrot of success, booting the football of hope towards the goals that we have set for ourselves somewhere on the level playing field of life.

All of which is well and good if that's the way you're made but not everyone is, or at least I'm not, and nor was Bill Vaughan. Bill Vaughan's dead but he used to write newspaper columns, one of which I read in the lavatory this morning and I discovered that Billyboy reckoned to spend, on average, twenty-seven minutes of every working day straightening paperclips.

And with those few words Bill Vaughan reached out from the grave and up through the plumbing and he seized me. That's the power of literature for you. He told me I was not alone. Here was a man I could do business with. Or rather here was a man I could do anything but business with.

For Bill Vaughan, bless his portable Olivetti, was a waster of time, a procrastinator, a ditherer, and so am I and I'll be damned before I think it a sin.

But there, look there on that word 'waster'. In that word you can sense the grim grey Zeitgeist worming into my consciousness and tinkling the little bell of guilt. Straightening paperclips, it says in its thin puritan whine, is wasting time.

But it isn't. Oh no, and here, bolstered by Bill, I set my standard in the ground and I shall not be moved. Though I fight till my knees buckle and my body sways, as long as I can stand I shall defend the art of wasting time. I have straightened a thousand paperclips and I shall not be ashamed. The French call paperclips trombones, but whatever you call them they are made for straightening.

The Zeitgeist says they are for clipping papers. The Zeitgeist says they are for attaching mission statements to strategic plans. But I see every straightened trombone as a tiny act of rebellion against the zealots of efficiency. And a paperclip once straightened can never be returned to its former condition. It can be used to scrape under fingernails, to carve doodles on the sticky patina of my desk, to probe into wads of earwax in a manner that has the busybodies from Occupational Safety and Health screaming into their filing cabinets, but never again will it clip papers.

Of course this issue is bigger than paperclips and Bill and I are not alone. Malcolm Muggeridge, he of the face like an ancient apple and the voice that crackled like canvas, he is of our company. He even called his autobiography *Chronicles of Wasted Time*. When Muggeridge left India after a stint at a university he found a wad of unmarked exam scripts in his bag. And as he steamed slowly towards England he sat in a deckchair at the stern of his ship and rigorously marked each script, writing marginal comments, totting up figures, and then when he was done with it, he tossed it over the side. You can only admire such pointlessness, such spectacular wasting of time.

And Philip Larkin too knew all about wasting time. He called it 'time torn off unused'. And furthermore it was Larkin who observed that it matters little what you do with time for 'however you use it, it goes'.

And I am happiest letting it trickle through my fingers. I love nothing better than to muse, to woolgather, to find an old newspaper in a drawer when looking for something else and to spend half a morning reading it, to stare out of windows, to throw sticks for dogs, to paddle in the shallows of thought. The world is various, and wasting time is simply to float in its variety, to accept it rather than to try to affect it.

In Evelyn Waugh's *Decline and Fall* there's a mad architect – anyone for pleonasm? – called Otto Silenus who reckons that people should be divided not by sex but by disposition. There are, he says, dynamic people and static people. I would call them doers and doodlers, and of the two types I would like to think I know who are the happier. Eleven beers please.

The sell-by chef

My career as a television chef began in what passes for a supermarket in the seaside town of Obscurity where I was living between jobs. A television director, scouting for talent with a hand-held camera, stopped me at the checkout.

'Show us your basket,' he ordered. I tilted the red plastic container towards the lens, and displayed the ordinary foodstuffs from which I would conjure something extraordinary by way of dinner.

'Zoom in on the bread,' said the director and the simplicity of a toast-slice loaf filled the frame. 'I like it,' said the director. 'Talk us through it.'

With a hint of a lisp and a smile that beguiled, I explained how bread which had reached its sell-by date was sold at half-price. 'Boys,' said the director, 'we've got a title.'

And thus 'The Sell-By Chef' was born and the gas flame of my fame was lit.

I led the crew home where they gasped at the unadorned ruggedness of my kitchen. I whistled the dogs to clean the bench then said simply, 'Ladies and gentlemen, let's cook.'

'Just roll 'em,' screamed the director to the

cameraman as I prised the plastic tab from the bread bag in a manner so practised that it looked easy and flicked it across the kitchen like the schoolboy that at heart I am and which I make no effort to conceal from the camera.

'Priceless,' said the director, 'they'll lap it up.' I delved into the bag, tossed the crust to the dogs, then held a rectangular slice up close to the camera's inquisitive lens. 'Bread,' I said.

Television is a visual medium. I gave not another word of explanation, as, with enthralling slowness, I folded the bread into the palm of my hand and closed my fist around its textured white heart, squeezing until a little tongue of compressed dough oozed like hesitant toothpaste from the interstice between my crunched pinkie and my palm.

'Sexy,' drooled the director.

Slowly, like a bud unfolding, I opened my hand to show what had once been a slice of ageing bread now compressed into something little larger than a golf ball with the texture of white playdough. Shreds of bread adhered to the skin of my hand.

'Dwell on it,' screamed the director to the cameraman. 'It's the perfect cover. For the book of the series.'

I nodded. He and I shared a wavelength.

I flung the golf ball to the dogs then hauled towards me the plump hump of my toaster. With a rattlesnake speed that took the camera by surprise I dropped a brace of slices into the slots and depressed the moulded black plastic tongue on the toaster's flank.

The camera tilted to my face. I smiled enigmatically. 'Ease,' I said, 'that's what it's all about, ease and zen. A great cook exudes calm. Everything is one. We are what we eat. Now come with me.' Without pausing I led them into the other room where I swept newspapers imperiously from the sofa, and lowered the cameraman on to a whoopee cushion.

Its resonant fart drew gales of delight from the director. 'You are the child in all of us,' he exulted, 'every mother's son, every young girl's bad-boy lover. You are *it*.'

I was the first to smell the smoke. But I refused to run. In the kitchen I grasped the handle of a fork which protruded from the depths of solidified fat in the frying pan. The pan rose, as if reluctant to relinquish ownership, then the fork came away with the sound of a boot leaving mud and the pan fell back on to the hob.

I plunged the fork into a flaming slice, tossed the bread in the air, caught it, patted it from hand to hand, laid it on the bench, then did it again. Thick was the butter that I smeared on each slice. It melted instantly into the charred bread. Thick, too, was the raspberry jam. I handed a slice to the director. The camera stayed with me, dwelt on my mouth.

'*Pain flambé au framboise*,' I said, quietly, understatedly, and I sank my young and perfect teeth into its smoking, butter-rich heart.

Prizing advice

Some while ago I took up golf and I wrote, 'Nothing in life has so confirmed my fear that I have reached middle age.' I apologize for quoting myself here but, more importantly, I apologize for being wrong. For five minutes ago a phone call proved me wrong. It seems that I am not in middle age; I am in old age. In shuffling slippers I have rounded the final corner in the great race and am tottering towards the tape before an empty grandstand. The timekeeper yawns, glances at his watch and cocks his finger above the button that says stop. I am as old and slow and wrinkled as a tortoise. I have a spine like a stick of chalk. I mumble through gums, suck eggs and snooze. Soon I shall snap like a water biscuit.

I know all this because the man who telephoned me, you see, was a school principal. Would I, he asked, care to address his school prize-giving?

I have seen school prize-givings. In thirty-something years in schools, a dozen of them spent learning little and twenty of them teaching less, I have seen them all. I have heard a swag of boring bishops. I have heard a herd of entrepreneurs, smug with suits and wise with wallets, returning to the scene of the crimes of childhood and telling lies. I have heard famous sportspeople mumble platitudes about passion and dedication and hard work paying off, and the need for that horror of horrors, goal-setting. I have heard the fat-chested cock of immodesty crow loud and long about yesterday. I have sat through a man telling 600 children that at the age of fifteen he suddenly developed an unquenchable fascination with parrots, the breeding and showing thereof, and he urged the children to do likewise. I have endured military men encrusted with medals for having sent younger men to their death, and I have heard them say that life is a battle and that it pays to have God on your side and a couple of tanks. I have heard them all and I have even, God help me, smiled politely at their jokes.

The children haven't. The children have yawned, fidgeted, stirred, scratched themselves, fingered the cigarettes in their pockets, eyed the exits manned by teachers with folded arms and have switched their brains into neutral and their ears into stops. And now they will yawn, fidget, stir, scratch, finger, eye and switch in front of me. And they are wise.

For to what does the mind of a crusty oldster turn when invited to address children? As inevitably as a weathervane turns to the wind, it turns to advice. And in no field of human endeavour has so much air been vibrated to so little purpose as in the giving of advice. Advice is a refugee; everyone wishes to pass it on but no one wishes to receive it.

And is the advice of the old worth listening to?

86

Are parrots, the breeding and showing thereof, the key to life? Do God and tanks make good allies? Is it wise to set goals? I do not think so. Nor do I think that in the years I have lived I have learned very much of value to pass on. I remain the ignorant fool I always was. I may walk more slowly and suffer worse hangovers, but I continue to make the errors I made as a child. I have just got better at hiding them. Character is destiny, said Novalis and I am with him. It's what happens to happen, said Larkin and I am with him.

And there, in those last two sentences, you have it. Over the years I have collected a few nuggets of other people's wisdom. I have not surveyed the map of my experience and seen the world afresh. I have just stumbled from hap to mishap, read a few books on the way and picked up some pretty phrases like a bright-eyed, dull-brained magpie.

But let us suppose otherwise. Let us suppose for the moment that I had the wisdom of the ages and the wit of David Lange. Would it profit the world that I went to the prize-giving, reared to my feet to insincere applause and cast my wisdom about me like grain to fall where it will, some of it lodging perhaps in the heads of a few of the little darlings dragooned into sitting in patient rows before me, and, having lodged, sprouting into a beacon that will guide them through the dark alleys of their lives to come? No, it would not, for three simple reasons: one is that grains cannot sprout into beacons, the second is that the children would not be listening and the third is that nobody acts on advice.

I know so. For in the twenty years of teaching I have dispensed tons of the stuff. I have run two boarding houses and sprayed advice about me like a fountain. None of it did any good. The most salutary experience occurred when a boy in Canada came to talk to me after the others had gone to bed. He brought with him a toothbrush. We chatted about the toothbrush, then he told me that his mother had multiple sclerosis. He told me that she was deteriorating. He told me that he was afraid that she would die. He cried. And I could think of nothing to say. When he had said what he had to say he left.

In the morning I sought out a colleague whose wisdom I valued. I told him what had happened. I told him how hopeless I had felt, how I'd found nothing to say, no advice to give.

The wise man told me that, on the contrary, I had done the best thing. I had listened and my silence was the best advice that I could give. And he was right, of course. And now that I think of that story I realize that, if nothing else, I have written my prize-giving speech.

Snakehitch

In a poem called 'Snake', D.H. Lawrence tells how, in the heat of the day, he went to a water trough to drink and found a snake there before him. The snake was venomous and Lawrence had to wait in line. I have always liked the poem, partly for the description of the slack-bellied snake and the precise way it sips at the water trough, but more for the way the poem ends.

Last night it was raining. I was driving up the motorway towards the Lyttelton tunnel having spent the evening playing pool in a garage and sipping at good beer, drinking it slowly like whisky, making the bottle last, because I would be driving home. My companions were a taxi driver who played flamboyantly and a slack-bellied Internet entrepreneur who was surprisingly diffident and warm of heart and who owned the pool table and the garage. I played lucky pool, beat them both several times and then we sat on plastic chairs to smoke and talk about God and literacy and race. It was a fine evening.

Beside the motorway a youth was hitching. He should not have been. The car ahead of me slowed.

When the youth ran towards it the car drove away, the kids in the back seat leaning out of the window in the rain to laugh at the hitchhiker. He raised fingers to them.

Because I did not learn to drive a car until I was twenty-eight, and because I travelled many thousands of miles by thumb, I always pick up hitchhikers unless their appearance scares me. I stopped. The youth was drenched and when he climbed into the front seat I could smell the beer on him. I asked him where he was going. Akaroa, I thought he said.

I was going only as far as Lyttelton. Akaroa was an hour of hilly backroads beyond. In such weather and at such a time of night the youth stood little chance of getting a lift. I told him so. He did not reply. I looked across and his eyes were closed.

I nudged him awake and said it all again.

'I've got all night,' he said. 'It's taken all day to get out of Hamilton.'

'Hamilton?'

'Got to get to Tokoroa. I live in Tokoroa,' he said, as if explaining to someone stupid. His eyes started to close again.

I was unsure what to do.

'You know you're in Christchurch, don't you?'

'Yeah,' he said, but he didn't.

I kept him talking through the tunnel. I did not want him falling asleep in the car. I felt discomfited, not by his peaceable drunkenness but by his unreason. I also knew that I should give him a bed for the night, breakfast in the bright morning and then send him on his way. But I didn't want to. I didn't want the inconvenience.

He said he was a student. Exams were in a fortnight. I asked him if he was running away from something but the question got no answer. I repeated that I was going only as far as Lyttelton where I lived. He said that was fine but I don't believe he heard me. My words were noise.

We came out of the tunnel and turned a corner and I stopped the car. He was fast asleep again. I nudged him and he asked me if we were in Tokoroa. I told him we were in Lyttelton and this was as far as I could take him. He fumbled a bit for the door catch and then got out and walked down the street. This side of the hills it was not raining but below the streetlights the wind of midnight billowed his shirt of red check. I watched him down the road. For a drunk he walked remarkably straight.

I drove home, greeted the dogs, checked for telephone messages and found I had none, then put my jacket back on, got back into the car and drove round Lyttelton to look for the youth and offer him a bed for the night. The bars had almost all closed. I couldn't find him. I wondered what he would be doing, whether he was curled in a garage or had found a lift further into confusion. I knew I had failed him. My selfishness had failed him and I felt guilt.

This morning the guilt is only a niggle. By tomorrow it will have gone.

At the end of the poem Lawrence threw a log at

the snake. Its tail writhed and it was gone and Lawrence was left with regret. He knew he had let himself down, had betrayed some sense of fitness, rightness.

'And I have something to expiate,' wrote Lawrence, 'a pettiness.'

Eyes right

The button that holds my trousers up came off so I went to the optician's.

The trousers in question are my default trousers, in other words the trousers I put on when I don't think about what trousers I am putting on. Made from corduroy the colour of algae they are so moulded to my shape that at night I don't so much take them off as step out of them and leave them standing on the bedroom floor like a pair of siamese sentries. In the morning I just step back into them and let them walk me to the coffee machine.

I don't blame my tailor for the lost button – I have had nothing but the best from Mr Hallenstein – instead I blame that thief of all things, time. Time has sucked my mighty shoulders south. If he keeps it up, by the year 2030 I'll look like the Pyramid of Cheops.

When I went to sew the button back on I found that time had also shrunk my arms. I could no longer hold a needle and thread far enough away for me to focus. Repeatedly I tried to pass a blur through a blur and repeatedly I sensed that I had failed in the same way as the witch in Macbeth sensed that evil was approaching, i.e. by the pricking of my thumbs.

Once or twice I did manage to thread the needle but I discovered my success only at the precise moment when I was parting my fingers to have another go and a fraction of a millisecond too late I felt the tiny resistance of the thread pulling through the eye of the needle like either a rich man or a camel. On the one occasion I did manage to stop with the needle threaded, requiring me only to seize the short end and pull it through, I seized the long end.

I could of course have used a magnifying glass, but a magnifying glass needs holding and I was already holding the thread, the needle and my breath.

Do you know the difference between an optician, a dispensing optician, an optometrist and an ophthalmologist? Nor do I, but they are all like trap-door spiders. The phonebook revealed that there were thousands of them out there, all previously unnoticed by me, waiting with the patience of time itself for the inevitable day that would bring me and my wallet stumbling into their den. I chose the optician who printed his phone number in 36-point type on the grounds that he seemed like a man who knew his market.

There is pleasure in submitting to expertise, in handing your problem over to a man who knows. My optician was charming, patient and ridiculously young. He reassured me that the eye-test wouldn't hurt. I hadn't expected it to hurt. Now I did. He swung lights around, presented me with charts and diagrams, fixed an extraordinary machine in front of my face and peered deep into my eyes in the way that lovers are meant to but in my experience don't unless they're psychotic or dogs.

And having tested all that my eyes could do he popped onto the bridge of my nose a pair of slotted lensless spectacles that looked as though they had been forged by a neolithic blacksmith and into one of the slots he dropped a lens and asked if that was any better and I said it was worse and he said good, and then he dropped another lens in front of it and then another and then another and suddenly all was as clear and bright as the first morning of spring, and in the manner of a man who had just performed a conjuring trick he asked if that was better now and I said yes it was and I was most impressed but I had been hoping for a horn-rimmed pair.

With the aid of a cross-section diagram of an eye, a diagram similar to one that I remembered copying into a school exercise book in the early seventies and labelling vitreous humour, aqueous humour, retina, iris, and Dave Collier's a Pratt, he explained that the lens in my eye was ageing. A baby can focus apparently on the tip of its nose – and from my limited acquaintance with babies it seems that most of them do – but gradually the eye stiffens and the focal length extends and forces us ultimately into the optician's lair.

The optician and I agreed that I could probably go a little while longer without glasses but we both knew as we said goodbye that it was really *au revoir*. He and time have got me on a thread and they can and will soon wind me in.

'Oh and by the way,' he said, as I went to close the door behind me.

'Yes?'

'Pull your trousers up.'

Messing

It is all very well to mess with ourselves, but when we mess with nature we get problems.

For example, my mate Pat's got a radioactive cat. The beast developed a growth in its thyroid so the vet injected it with a substance that makes it glow in the dark. I should feel sympathy for the mog but, as with most misfortune, I find it funny, and besides it's one of those cats that expresses affection by biting.

The vet isolated the thrumming cat for a few days in a lead-lined cage but now that it's back at home it has to be locked out at night so that it doesn't sneak on to Pat's pillow and make him grow a second head. So instead it wanders luminously over the neighbour's roof, warping the corrugated iron and alarming the passing drunks.

Each morning Pat scans the yellowing vegetation of his garden with a Geiger counter, finds the beast and lets it into the house. But if he falls asleep on the sofa and wakes with the thing on his lap he has to take a two-hour shower and check his sperm count. One million and one, one million and two. . . .

Now luminosity hinders hunting, so I doubt if

Pat's cat at present is much good at catching birds, but I expect it gives them a fright. My own cat, however, which to my knowledge has never been radioactive, is in mid-season hunting form. Only this afternoon I found it torturing a sparrow with the sort of glee that I find it hard to like. Had there been any point in doing so I would have rescued the sparrow but I was already too late by a matter of several organs. The sparrow still tried to flutter away but aerodynamically it was a gone possum.

Five minutes later the cat brought me the tubular remains and rubbed against me in search of praise which I refused to give. Indeed, right now if my cat developed a dicky thyroid I don't think I'd fork out for the plutonium.

On the day I acquired my three chickens the cat stalked them. Ten metres from the coop it slunk down into that low-bellied crawl which it learned from David Attenborough, and then spent the best part of an hour sneaking up on the unwitting chooks across the lawn. On my lawn that's no great feat. In a recent gale my dustbin blew away – not much to my regret because its lid had always stuck and now I had the excuse to buy a green deluxe model from The Warehouse – but as soon as I'd replaced it I stumbled on the old bin which had been hiding in the depths of the lawn.

So the cat in the lawn was like a pedestrian in Manhattan, but still it stole towards the chickens with extraordinary caution, moving each limb separately with a rapt and sinuous malice. Eventually it parted the grass at the edge of the coop, beheld the chooks clearly for the first time, saw that each bird was twice its size, stared at them in a wild surmise then promptly lost interest.

Since then two chickens have gone broody, which means that they spend their days trying to hatch the eggs they haven't got. If the one active chook lays an egg the broodies fight over it until I take it away. Broody chooks don't lay and since they've nothing to rear I was keen to snap them from their broodiness. Pat of the luminous cat told me that one way to do it was to toss the chickens into the air.

So every day for the last two weeks I've tossed my chickens. As I reach into the nesting boxes the broodies swell like puffer fish, cluck weakly in protest and peck at my hands, but once they've been tossed and have fluttered back to earth and stood for a while to reorder brains the size of paper-clips, they suddenly remember that they are chickens and peck madly at grain and grass and swig beakfuls of water. Then they go back to their brooding till it's tossing time again.

Confronted with the failure of the tossing gambit I consulted the Internet. In ten minutes I had found a website called Fowlnews where I joined the hugely popular 'Poultry Information Exchange' and posted my problem on its virtual bulletin board. I expect you saw it.

Anyway, within the hour I had received several bits of virtual advice. Among them came an e-mail from a chicken-fancier known as Buzz from Wisconsin. Buzz told me that it is sometimes possible to snap chickens out of broodiness by scaring them. I'm going to borrow Pat's cat.

PS. I thank the correspondent who asked whether my phrase 'black women's shoes' in a recent column was the result of illiteracy or racism. I would love to plead illiteracy but I must admit to racism. I should of course have written 'Afro-American women's shoes'. I apologize to all whom I offended.

On noticing the shags

It is a law of life, or at least it is a law of my life, that you don't notice something until someone draws your attention to it. And as soon as they do draw your attention to it, you can't stop noticing it. For example, if someone says that it's been a good year for the yellow-bellied shag, I say 'What?'

'The yellow-bellied shag,' they say. 'Look.'

I look and what do I see but shags in all directions, diving and swooping on flowers and fish, their yellow bellies gleaming in the sun.

'Oh, of course, the yellow-bellied shag,' I say. 'I thought you said Macquarie Island shag', but all the time I am marvelling at how I missed all those shags – though at my age that is not an uncommon thought. But now I see shags everywhere, their bellies as yellow as butter.

But the converse of the shag theory is also true – if you pay no attention to something it isn't there. It is the ostrich theory. Ostriches famously hide by sinking their heads into sand. If they can't see the enemy, the enemy doesn't exist.

Ostriches have taken a lot of stick for this manoeuvre – not least from their enemies, and not always pleasantly – but in fact ostriches are wise birds. More often than not, if you hide from something it does go away. If, for example, you don't turn on the news the government disappears. And the same seems to be true of tonsils.

Last year my tonsils mutinied. Immediately I became a tonsil bore and discovered that everyone, but everyone, had a tonsil story that had previously lain buried beneath my lack of interest. It seemed that the whole world pulsed with tonsils.

My tonsils proved instructive. After skirmishing for a few weeks they went properly to war. They hurled infections at me. I lobbed penicillin back, but the infections skulked like Chechen rebels in the rugged crevices of Tonsilland, waited for the antibiotic cloud to pass, then rose again revitalized to wage the war afresh. Eventually they sent me to hospital where the nurses wheeled out the serious artillery. They injected stuff into me. They dripped stuff into me. The infections came out with their hands up like germs in a toilet cleaner ad. I left the hospital with a song in my heart and youth in my throat.

But the hospital knew more about tonsils than I. They told me that once a tonsil had turned treacherous, it could never be trusted to be a loyal citizen again. It might doff its cap as the monarch passed, but all the while it would be fingering the knife in its belt and muttering words of treason.

'We have scotched the snake,' said the doctors, 'not killed it. Have those tonsils out and be done with it.'

I have never undergone surgery. I would prefer not to undergo surgery but I accepted.

Well, soon afterwards the hospital sent me a nice letter. It said that the condition of my tonsils earned me fifty points. It was a bit like air miles. In the present state of waiting lists fifty points entitled me to have my operation at no time in the foreseeable future. If, however, my condition improved and I no longer needed the operation I couldn't have, would I be kind enough to let them know so that they could slot someone else into my place in the list to wait for it.

'Sure,' I said and promptly did an ostrich. It worked. I forgot about my tonsils and my tonsils forgot about me. Effectively they ceased to exist.

That was six healthy months ago. Last week the hospital rang me in exultant form. They had got more money. They could take my tonsils out whenever I wished. I said I didn't wish. God, I said, had joined me and my tonsils together and let no man put us asunder. Besides, I said, they didn't hurt any more.

'Well done,' said the hospital, 'bravo', and we parted on terms of mutual praise. I said they were a nice hospital and they said I was a clever little tonsil conqueror.

That night I dreamt that my tonsils hurt. The next morning they did. The morning after that they hurt some more. I rang the hospital.

'You know that tonsil business,' I said.

'We were waiting for you to call,' they said. In the background I caught the sound of scalpels being sharpened.

103

I am sure that if the hospital hadn't reminded me of them my tonsils would have behaved. The mind, it seems, has a mind of its own. And now I sit at my desk, looking out of the window, dreading the pain of a tonsillectomy and barely noticing the swooping and chortling of a flock of yellow-bellied shags.

This is terribly emotional

Last week was National Poetry Week or Day or something, but whatever it was the wise went into hiding. Only now that it's over are the wise emerging from their underground shelters, blinking at the sunlight and still looking nervously around in case some character in a home-knitted jersey with stains should shamble up to them and fix them with his glittering eye and start reading from a slim volume.

At university I learned all about these amateur poetry johnnies. They used to lurk in bars, always in sensitive jerseys, some even polo-necked, their shaking pianist's fingers clutching half-pints of mild beer from which they never drank. The jerseys and the untouched beer should have been warning enough but these people were cunning.

They would take an intense interest in that most permanently interesting of subjects, me. I would say something and they would lean across the table and say 'Oh really', and gaze at me with spaniel eyes, 'Oh really, that's terribly interesting', which of course it was because I had said it. And as I was young and easy under the apple bough, I fell for their flattery like any honest housewife for a brush salesman.

The jersey-wearing poets probably had a little manual for snaring suckers like me, a manual explaining just how to sit in bars looking empathetic, how to draw me in to spit out all the butt ends of my days and ways, in short, how to soften me up before moving in for the kill. And because I could not discern the difference between interest in me – which was admirable – and feigned interest in me – which was inconceivable – I fell for it every time.

Oh there was warning enough, but I was blind to the signs. For a while all would go swimmingly. I would deliver a Bennett monologue eloquent with grief, surrendering my heart of anger to the stranger, and punctuated only by the jersey's tuts and moans of sympathy, but then the conversation would take a subtle and ominous turn. The 'How you've suffered, my dear', which was both gratifying and bang on, would become 'My dear, how we've suffered', which was neither. At that point I should, of course, have reared to my feet, swallowed the half-pint of mild in a single gulp, tossed the glass over my shoulder, proclaimed that no coward soul was mine and stalked imperious and alone into the great night of self-pity. But I never did.

Soon afterwards the shutters would fall on the bar like a prison door slamming with me on the wrong side of it, and I would be out on the street with the jersey, and somehow, imperceptibly, the conversation would turn on its head. Instead of speaking I would find myself listening, an activity which is rarely wise and never pleasant, and then inevitably there came the fateful invitation. The jersey's rooms were just around the corner and would I, perhaps, care to round off the evening with a little drink? In the hope of scotch I would follow. The consequences were unspeakable and the scotch always, but always, turned out to be cocoa.

But worse, far worse, than the cocoa was the poetry. How did I never see it coming? Oh beat at this pate that let this folly in and my poor judgment out, but soon I would be sunk in an armchair and the jersey would be sunk in another and he – it was nearly always he, though once or twice and every bit as horribly it wasn't – would reach for a cloth-bound notebook and with an 'I thought perhaps you might like . . .' he would open it and cough and start to read and I would be a possum in the headlights.

The poetry was ghastly. It was all love and death and skeletal trees and mossy thighs and sagging fenceposts, but worse even than the poetry was the voice. You know the poetry reading voice, the this-is-terribly-emotional voice, all hushed and reverential. You can still hear it sometimes on the radio. It is the voice of undressing for non-sexual purposes, the voice of the guidance counsellor after a yoga session, bowel-twisting, precious, breathy, earnest and wrong. It turns my spine to chicken skin.

There would be nothing I could do. The poet chap would have me sprawling on a pin. When finally I escaped after what seemed like years I would run through the night, drawing lungfuls of air and shouting my horror to the skies, and when finally I regained my rooms I would collapse with relief on my bed. Beside the bed a dusty table. On the table a cloth-bound notebook. Inside the notebook, well, how do you take your cocoa?

Too *many eggs*

I have long maintained that cooked food comes in only two types: recognizable and unrecognizable. Recognizable food looks like what it started as. Examples include steak, sausages and goats' heads. All recognizable food is best fried, of course, except for goats' heads, which should be boiled slowly with garlic, bay leaves and balsamic vinegar and then thrown away.

A friend who made the strange decision to woo a Spanish woman was once fed goat's head by his prospective in-laws. Apparently the best part of a goat's head is the gums. The only way to get at the gums is to gnaw. My friend is not a squeamish man – he is Scottish and he likes football – but he confessed to finding it a trial to watch, and hear, his fiancée clashing teeth with a goat. It took, he said, the bloom from romance.

Anyway, because I cook for myself my diet consists entirely of recognizable food. It is only when I eat out that I graze on unrecognizable food, which is defined as stuff cooked by other people in which the ingredients are not imme-diately evident. Examples of unrecognizable food are cake, hollandaise sauce and everything Indian.

All of which serves only to introduce my egg problem. I have too many eggs. Spring has triggered some biological alarm clock in my chickens' tiny minds, and their ovary ducts are working like the plastic gun which I was given for Christmas when I was six and which fired ping-pong balls at relatives with a gratifying velocity. (Of course, it was the ping-pong balls rather than the relatives which showed the velocity, although when my only aunt copped a beauty in the back of the neck she moved with a swiftness that a glance at her ankles would have suggested was improbable.)

My eggs are splendid things, as dense as a parcel of protons, and I have cooked them in as many ways as I know how, but even I have tired of fried eggs. And although I have given away as many eggs as I can to both my friends I am still embarrassed by a superfluity.

The woman who knows suggested I cook quiche. I realize, of course, that real men don't eat quiche but I love it, and I don't care if it wreaks havoc on my wrists.

The woman who knows assured me quiche was easy. But it requires pastry. I have never done pastry. And when I wrenched Delia Smith from the library I found that she devoted six pages to pastry. I read them with horror. There was a paragraph called 'pastry psychology' and another called 'pastry perversity'. And, most puzzlingly of all, I learned that good pastry requires cold hands.

Lacking a thermometer, I headed for the super-market where I found an agreeably cheap chunk of ready-made pastry the colour and consistency of a corpse. When I dropped it on the kitchen bench the thud frightened the dogs.

As a child I had seen my mother rolling pastry. She made it look easy. But my mother never tried to roll pastry with a bottle of Queen Adelaide Regency red. The neck of the bottle proved a satisfactory handle. The base of the bottle didn't. And proper rolling pins don't come with a label bearing an embossed picture of Queen Adelaide. Perhaps they should. My pastry was soon dotted with little reverse pictures of Her Majesty which further rolling distorted into hall-of-mirrors monstrosities. It proved rather enjoyable in a republican sort of way.

Transferring the pastry to the pan that would serve as a quiche dish was the sort of activity that makes me grateful that my kitchen is not rigged with surveillance cameras. The dogs prospered. But eventually and after a fashion all was done, and I prodded the pastry into corners and pricked it and baked it blind as Delia told me I should, and I mixed up a pint of cream and a mound of cheese and a foothill or two from my egg mountain, and I poured the sludge into the half-baked pastry and then sat with a fistful of Queen Adelaide to watch my creation become quiche. And it did so with such success that I dined on it for four days running and the dogs grew plump on the burned bits of crust.

And when, out of gratitude, I tossed the final sliver of quiche to the chickens, they sank their beaks into their thwarted genetic inheritance with every appearance of glee. Unrecognizable cooking? I rest my case.

Lie lie lie

As every schoolboy knows – no, that won't do. We can't say that phrase any more. For a start we can't say schoolboy, implying as it does that there's a difference between the sexes – and we can't say sexes either because it inflames their adolescent passions. The truth, of course, is that the only thing that makes adolescence even remotely tolerable is that there *is* a gulf between the sexes and that hormones widen it by the hour and that inflammation is fun. But truth is out of fashion.

We can't say schoolchildren either, because it demeans the little darlings. It defines them by their youth and by the place that is failing to educate them, and thus tramples on their frail self-esteem.

No, we have to call them students and so induct them into the modern world by giving them their very own first little lie to play with. Students study. Now go spy on the teenage bags of testosterone barrelling and boasting down the street when school is out about five minutes past midday on a weekday afternoon and try to imagine them doubled over a book.

Nevertheless, as every student knows – no, you

see, it still won't do, the problem being that you can't rely on them knowing anything. The whole grab bag of chunks of literature and gobbets of knowledge that used to be considered indispensable has been hurled from the third-floor window of the teachers' training college. All truth has become relative and we have become scared of misleading youth and thus we condemn the little sweeties to a life of fumbling guiltless rootless discontent.

But there is one thing that we can teach tomorrow's citizens before plucking them from the teat of education and tossing them into the wicked world to make what way they can. We can teach them how to respond to telephone surveys. More precisely we can teach them what to do when they're heating a tin of sausages and baked beans and the phone rings and a woman asks to speak to the person in the house who is over the age of eighteen and who buys instant coffee.

The options, of course, are several of which the most obvious and appealing is to be staggeringly rude. It is the wrong option.

The right option is to whoop 'That's me, honeybun, you're talking to him', crook the phone between ear and shoulder, tip the beans and sausages on to a plate and prepare to tell lies. Lying to questionnaires is everyone's duty as a free-born citizen. It's enormous fun and it distracts attention from the sheer awfulness of the beans and sausages. Have you seen those sausages? There are about four to a tin and each is the colour and size of the severed finger of a drowned dwarf. But not the texture. Oh no, the texture is of goat's brain, parboiled with a pinch of gelatine.

The survey woman will ask you to rank each of the following brands of instant coffee on a scale of one to five, where five means you would crawl over burning hymnbooks to get a sniff of it and one means that you wouldn't touch it with asbestos gloves. Now's the time to lie. Tell the most monstrous whoppers. Confess a passion for that appalling powdered parody coffee that tastes like an old people's home in New Plymouth.

But be sweet to the woman who is asking the questions. It is not her fault that she's landed with the job from Dreadsville. She's stuck at home with the kids and she's got no money. The people who have got the money are the slab-faced executives who grind up the New Plymouth old folks' home and try to convince you with execrable and mendacious advertising that the stuff is drinkable.

Play them at their own game. One glance at their advertising confirms that they think the public has a delta minus brain that can be duped by pictures of a svelte woman cradling a steaming cup of their horrorbroth which is solely responsible for her having got her hands on a hunk of a hubby, two cherubic children and some nauseating furniture. Confirm their misconception. The questions asked will be transparent. Tell them what they want to hear. Convince them their advertising works. Lie lie lie.

With any luck the result will be a preposterously expensive advertising campaign based on the survey,

114

a campaign that will lose them a lot of money. And so, because you have spent ten minutes lying down the phone, the survey woman will get paid, you won't notice the taste of the sausages and someone in head office might just click that telephone surveys are an unconscionable invasion of privacy. In other words, everyone's a winner – which, as it happens, is one of the few things that every modern schoolboy knows.

Room

I write this in bed in the afternoon in the country in winter in a motel room that looks like the administrative office of Pukesville, Sadship and Grimm.

T. S. Eliot wrote of restless nights in one-night cheap hotels. Eliot didn't know the half of it. His hotels had sawdust floors and oyster shells. My motel has a carpet that can damage the retina.

The country in these parts is flat, empty and wet. The motel room is worse. It just doesn't bear thinking about. Yet I am thinking about it. I don't want to think about it. I don't want to write about it. But it empties the mind of all thoughts except razor blades. This is the motel where decor came to die. It makes me want to spit out all the butt-ends of my days and ways. And how shall I begin?

Vertebrae C1 to C6 are screaming. I have wedged the two Ethiopian charity-case pillows under the small of my back where they have burrowed irretrievably between the wall and the end of the thing that the proprietor would no doubt call a mattress. The weight of my chest, head, trapezoids, deltoids, pecs, abs and other flab is applied through the back of my head against the sort of floral wallpaper that is made out of recycled Bulgarian ration books and which the health departments of better countries banned in 1953. And that's the pretty wall. The other walls are concrete blocks painted regurgitation pastel.

The bed is covered with a ridged nylon bedspread the colour of something that needs to be drained. In an effort to shield my eyes from it I have littered the bedspread with the 7000 sections of the Sunday newspaper which focus on real estate and an activity called Living. Living seems to mean quilting clubs in the Manawatu, novels by women with armpits, the recipe for a Peruvian sardine dish with chives, and scrofular adolescents from Glasgow who are pleased to call themselves a 'band'. If that's Living I want nothing to do with it. And there isn't enough of it to cover the bedspread.

I am on the bed because I am not at the table. The table is worse than the bed. The table is in marble-finish formica, of course, on tubular chrome, of course, and it is littered with brochures for activities that would traumatize the dead. You can visit the new seed-drill display at the art and craft museum, tour the historic woolshed or trek with a spavinned pony. Against the table stand two chairs of chrome and plastic which attracted no bidders at the sort of auction attended by people with trackpants and limps.

The bathroom contains neither a bath nor room. The walls weep. The shower would scald the bristles off a pig and then freeze it for later. It will

117

do nothing in between. And you couldn't fit a pig into it anyway. The thin nylon curtain stays cold under hot water and clings to wet flesh like a squid. It thinks it's a towel, except it doesn't dry you. Nor do the towels. The towels are sandpaper.

It is easy to enter the toilet by simply sucking in the stomach, flattening oneself against the weeping wall and shuffling sideways. I have just swung a cat in the toilet and killed it instantly. Had it been able to, it would have thanked me. The cat will never have to return to the kitchenette to see the plastic salt cellar or the patterned plates or the unused potato masher in the drawer that sticks.

Tomorrow morning the cat will not have to face the continental breakfast that comes from no continent yet inhabited by mankind. That breakfast will be delivered to the door on a plastic tray by the proprietor and will comprise a bowl of four canned apricots, two slices of rectilinear suet bread, and individual portions of a polyunsaturated spread that tastes of desperation.

No doubt lots of motels are fine places. The last one I stayed in had milk in glass bottles, a heater that heated, tolerable furniture and a television that I eventually managed to turn on.

But this place sears the soul. And I haven't even mentioned the pictures on the walls. Nor am I going to. I haven't the words. You'll have to imagine them. And besides, I've decided to leave. I'm going home to soothe the soul with dogs and T. S. Eliot.

Bronzino, the brat and the bird

A psychiatrist has just sent me a postcard from Florence. All postcards carry the same message: Having a wonderful time. Glad you're not here. Love from the hamster who's left the cage. P.S. Please feel envy.

I do envy the psychiatrist but I am also grateful to her. Her postcard has introduced me to the fat brat.

The fat brat is 455 years old. In 1545 he was painted in all his fatness by a chap called Bronzino. At the time Bronzino was forty-two and the fat brat was about eighteen months.

The brat is so fat that his knuckles are dimples. In the cross-eyed manner of infants he is staring at the painter and gurgling with plump pleasure. At any moment he will dribble. The dribble will fall on a doublet of velvet. The cloth's as thick as a wad of money and the colour of raspberries and its seams are sewn with gold thread.

The brat's left hand dangles empty. The right clutches a goldfinch. The bird is clearly alive but the brat is far too self-satisfied to pay it attention. But Bronzino has paid the bird attention. With a skill detectable even on a postcard he has captured the tiny curve of its beak, the scarlet splash of its face, the black hood like a cowl and the slash of gold across its wings which lends the bird its name.

My grandfather had a goldfinch. I remember it on Saturday afternoons hopping in apparent boredom between the two perches in its cage while my grandfather smoked and watched horse racing on a black and white television in a darkened room and my grandmother sucked Imperial mints. I was as bored as the bird. Goldfinches sing like metallic water but I do not remember hearing this bird sing.

Bronzino got the goldfinch right. From the window as I write I can see goldfinches on a telephone wire. The birds perch briefly in ones and twos, allowing me a glimpse of their nervous brilliance. I see the scarlet face, the startling bands of gold. I glance from the postcard to the birds, a distance of four and a half centuries. Nothing's changed. Then the goldfinches scatter. They fly in pulses, like little heartbeats. Sometimes on the Port Hills I see huge mobs of goldfinches pecking at the seed-tufts of thistles or clinging to the swaying stems of grasses. When I scare them they rise like a tiny storm and clamour.

And just as he captured the goldfinch Bronzino captured the child and all he stood for. You can sense from the painting that the infant mouth is stuffed with silver spoons. For though the child's Christian name was plain Giovanni, his surname was Medici.

The Medicis ruled Florence for 300 years. The first Medici made money from banking, turned his florins into power and then handed it down. Some of his descendants ruled as tyrants and made a lot more money. Others didn't and didn't. From the way little Giovanni is clutching the goldfinch I fancy he would have prospered.

Three Medicis became pope and one, Lorenzo the Magnificent, magnificently made his son a cardinal at the age of fourteen. That trinity of blood ties, money and power is as old as history. It goes on. You could see it in the stands in the Olympic opening ceremony. There sat poor Chelsea Clinton like a Medici child. There sat Bill Gates the Magnificent grinning like a strange one.

The Medicis were patrons of the arts. They sponsored not only Bronzino but also Leonardo and Michelangelo. They wanted themselves and their offspring and their glory recorded by the best talent they could buy. They bought, in short, immortality.

But just as the goldfinch goes on, and the dynasties of power go on, so, too, does irony. 500 years ago the Medicis built an office block from which to run their government more efficiently, and the building still stands. Its use, however, has changed. Today it is the Uffizi Gallery. When the psychiatrist visited Florence it was the first place that she went to, along with a million others. She went to pay homage, but not to the Medicis.

For when the tourists stare at the painting of the double-chinned child it is not Giovanni Medici that they see. What they see is what Bronzino saw, the Medicis as they were, smug with power and superfluous wealth. And, transcending every Medici who ever lived, they see the durability of art and the brilliance of a bird.

Indeed the Uffizi is like a postcard to the past. 'Dear Medicis,' it reads, 'Weather in the twenty-first century wonderful. Sorry you couldn't join us. But your hireling Bronzino is here and in very good form. He sends his regards. Love, Time.'

Call me Goodness

Filthy evening, tooling home in my filthy car, dogs purring, engine humming, something French and croony on the radio, heater toasting the toes, lights refracted through the windscreen rain, all that sort of stuff, when I perceive distress. Distress on the near side of the road in the form of a stopped car and a drenched youth. So drenched indeed that as the cars sprayed past with that tyres-on-wet-tarseal noise that is so beloved of advertisers who want to contrast the nasty urban winter with the comforts of home and 600 channels of pornography and a cup of synthetic soup, the regulation knee level crotch of this youth's jeans had sunk even to his ankles.

Naturally my first reaction was to chortle. Everything about the image was delightful: pampered ignorant urban youth being delivered a lesson in hubris. As I drew alongside him I did the decent thing, nudging the wheel sightly to the left in order to drench him further. Revenge for all the times he and his like have roared up my street with their unnecessary horsepower and made me seethe.

Ten yards past I stopped. I don't know why, by which I mean I know perfectly well why. Like every good samaritan including the Good Samaritan I just wanted to think well of myself. Having the mechanical nous of a fish I was unlikely to be of any practical use to the youth with the dead car, but I was certain to be of immense use to myself. If I stopped to help I would feel virtuous.

The child had skin the colour of pastry, illuminated by little carmine eruptions of acne. His hair hung in sodden wisps and his bright cotton clothes were comically inadequate. Here in all its unglory was the progeny of a decadent age, a youth whose only previous notion of misfortune was a lack of narcotics or having to do some work.

He also had one of those cars which I'd be happy to bazooka – phallic bonnet, low-slung passenger pod and a spoiler carved from testosterone. And doubtless the muffler had been removed or punctured to create noise. Quite how these children acquire these monsters I don't know. Maybe their parents give them to them in the hope they'll drive away until they grow up. But anyway this noxious car was dead. It had no fuel.

Its owner's manner was all resentment at the gross unfairness of the world and at the petrol attendant half a mile up the road who had apparently refused to exchange the youth's last $5 for petrol because he had nothing to carry the petrol in. Nor would the attendant lend him a can without a deposit of $10.

I didn't have a petrol can. Nor did I have a syphon. But I did have a wallet. It held, I knew, a single $20 note.

Call me squidgy-hearted, call me a sentimental

fool, call me the quintessence of virtue. You would be wrong on all counts. I gave him the $20 because I wanted to get out of the rain.

But even the appearance of virtue brings rewards. The moment that I drew the wallet from my pocket the youth was transformed. He became a moral being. He backed away. He held up a hand. He said no. He held up both his hands. He didn't want my money.

I pressed him to take it.

'I'll pay it back,' he said, as at last he took it, as if only by saying the words, by voicing his virtuous intentions, could he justify accepting the charity.

And I knew then that he would indeed pay me back and I told him that I knew, and I gave him a lift up the road to the petrol station and he was charming and effusive and he wrote down my name and address and he told me time and time over that he always paid his debts, and when finally he got out armed with my money, I liked him. I drove home singing.

I was pleased by my own sense of goodness but more by having uncovered goodness in another, and particularly in one so intractable and young. Beneath the snarl of this unprepossessing adolescent lay the old near-instincts of pride and independence and a sense of obligation and a sense of gratitude. It did not make me weep, but it did make me happy, to know that the old stuff still rolled in the human heart. The world was not a bad place. It was still the right way up.

I should point out that this is not a recent story. It happened last winter. Twelve months on and I still haven't heard from the little sod.

A castle of teeth

I envy my dogs their perfect white teeth. Those teeth look like the Southern Alps and their gums look like Ashburton – by which I mean that they are as pink and healthy as the rural economy.

The dogs' dental hygiene regime consists of eating anything that comes to paw. Perhaps the secret of their impeccable teeth lies in the bones that they gnaw each morning, because they brush those teeth about as often as I bark.

It seems a bit unfair, then, that after forty years of diligent brushing my own teeth look nothing like the Southern Alps. If they resemble anything it is a thirteenth-century Scottish castle. The battlements have been holed by sudden assaults and slow erosion. Ugly patchings mar the original stonework which has itself been stained by time, tempest and coffee. My teeth are the colour of a lizard's belly and as frail as sun-bleached plastic. Perhaps I should have chewed a daily bone.

Though tourists may hike to Scottish castles and point their Kodaks at the ruins, the only camera ever tilted at the crenellations of my mouth is the blunt-nosed X-ray monster that dangles from the dentist's ceiling like a smooth and alien root vegetable. The dentist nuzzles the vegetable against my cheek, shrouds me in a cook's apron of lead, assures me that there's nothing to worry about and takes cover behind three insulated walls and a plump hygienist.

Nothing to worry about, that is, until the vegetable delivers its verdict on my mouth in the form of ghost-grey negatives, medical holiday snaps that strip away the irrelevance of flesh to show the truth of bone. I see my Yorick jaw. The dentist sees something else. That molar, he says, and his head wobbles involuntarily from side to side in the universal gesture of regret as he holds the album of my mouth to the light of the window so that any passing pedestrian can glimpse my oral decline. The whole world tuts.

I have been drilled more than the North Sea. I have more fillings than a pie factory. I do not want to be drilled or filled again. Nor do I want to gum my way through the twenty-first century, nor fish my smile each morning from a bedside glass. So, though perhaps it is too late, I have decided to act. I have formed a sort of historic places trust for my teeth. And the first decision of the newly formed trust was to protect as far as was practicable, and with a mind to the limited resources at its disposal, the existing remnants of my tooth castle.

Once what was left was stabilized then we could proceed to restoration – some intricate bridgework perhaps, a sliver of gold leaf, some artificial crowns. But first we had to stick a standard in the ground of my gums and declare that past this point there would be no retreat. What little we still have we shall defend. So I bought an electric toothbrush.

How in more thoughtless years I would have scoffed at that purchase. I would have called it a consumer bauble, a gewgaw, a frippery. But, said the dentist, if I were to buy this toothbrush the days of plaque would be over. Never again would he have to take the scraper to my enamel with its nails-on-blackboard screeching, never again would he wheel out the batsqueak ultra-sonic device with its shattering hot-cold squeal. And my teeth would blanch and blossom. You're on, I said.

I chose the deluxe model – wall-mounted, pulsing and oscillating, variable speed, automatic two-minute timer, double overhead cam and wishbone suspension front and rear.

Novelty always excites me. For though I like putting few things in my mouth apart from food, fingernails and the stems of grasses, and although electrical goods are a particular no no, nevertheless I fair sprinted to the bathroom to test my sleek new $90 of dental gadgetry. My hands trembled as I smeared a snail of paste across the virgin bristles and I pressed the button called ON. Those hands were still trembling as I pressed the button called OFF and wiped the spray of toothpaste from the mirror.

I consulted the manual, smeared another snail, laid the brush against a lower back tooth and set the thing in motion. It felt like a bumble bee on a stick. And when I switched to the upper jaw my whole skull resonated in a sort of Wagnerian drone. And behind it all like hushed percussion the pitter-patter of falling plaque.

My bathroom overlooks my garden. Glancing from the window, brush in mouth, I caught sight of the dogs gnawing at bones. Our eyes met. We winked at each other, knowingly, and grinned. I felt the spring sun glint.

Standing for nothing

I know my godson's name but he does not know mine. Shortly after he was born I sent him a present but he didn't write back so that was the end of that. But I have just learned that if his parents should perish in a car crash I will become responsible for my godson's moral education. Poor little darling. I wish his parents long and happy lives and I suggest they buy a Volvo.

My relationship with my godson resembles my relationship with God. Once or twice in times of stress I've tried to ring God but he hasn't answered the phone. I have spoken only to his secretary, Miss Time, an ancient spinster, all bosom and tweed. Miss Time always tells me that God's in a meeting and asks if she could be of help. I unburden myself to her and she offers unchanging advice. 'Wait,' she says, 'be patient. This too will pass.' She's right, of course, but it always takes a while for things to get better and by then I can't be bothered to write and thank her. In which respect, I suppose, I'm as ungrateful as my godson. But actually I prefer Miss Time to God. God's too definite for me. He's got strong opinions.

I once knew a school chaplain who wore short shorts and read short prayers. Children, he said, paid little attention to long prayers. I could have told him that they paid scant attention to any prayers, but I didn't because, well, I just didn't. Anyway, his favourite prayer ran thus: 'O Lord, let me stand for something lest I fall for anything. Amen.'

This prayer impressed me by its brevity, its memorability, its neat antithetical construction and its profound and unmatchable stupidity. It suggests that any opinion is better than no opinion. It suggests that having no opinion is dangerous. The truth of the world is precisely the opposite. Opinions are bad things.

By opinions I do not mean ideas, and I do not mean thought. An opinion is rarely born of thought. Instead it arrives fully formed in a head. Opinions are, as I have written elsewhere, almost always emotion in fancy dress. They can be inherited, or they can spring from fears or desires, but they are never right.

Yet look how ferociously, how indefatigably, people cling to their opinions in the face of a flood of evidence that those opinions are at best questionable, and more likely mere dump fodder.

Look at the intransigent folly of so much politics. Look at the nonsense that passes for political debate. Listen to the roaring when a political opponent slips. Hear the deep delighted belly laughs when the minister gets confused. That isn't debate. That's merely a primal contest for power in which one side has caught a glimpse of an unprotected jugular. Yet if you want to take part in this contest you are required to join a team and in order to join a team you have to have a packaged set of opinions.

Where do those opinions come from? Are they arrived at by rational analysis? If so, and if reason is reason, how come they differ? But opinions are not reasonable.

We are emotional creatures in an irrational world. Anyone who holds opinions is wrong and dangerous. The European colonists of the nineteenth century were wrong and dangerous. Karl Marx was wrong and dangerous. George Speight is wrong and dangerous.

The only comfortable seat for a thinking human being is a fence. How is it, when we know so much about human nature from Shakespeare's plays, know more indeed than we could hope to garner from any other source, that we know so little about Shakespeare's opinions? The answer is that he doubted. He was a fence-sitter, an observer, a puppeteer who jigged his little figures about on stage and made them hold every opinion which was popular in the sixteenth century – and which, oddly enough, are the same opinions as are popular in the twenty-first – and he set his opinionated characters to play out their dramas of conflict and resolution, of crowns and thorns, of love and loss, of birth and death while he himself sat in among them smiling gently, tolerantly on their fierce little blindnesses. Shakespeare knew the primacy of emotion and the supreme virtue of doubt.

So if my buddy God should move in that

mysterious way of his and drop a thunderbolt or a tree on the Volvo that belongs to my old friends Philip and Olivia and thereby squash them dead, then I shall indeed accept the duty of a godfather. And when I greet my grief-stricken godson at the airport, I shall straightway seize him by the ankles and shake him until all opinions tumble out of him. And I shall then endeavour to fill the gap with doubt.

And, as has always been the way of the world, and as will always be the way of the world, the boy won't listen to a word I say. Just like everybody else, he will have to nose his own way through Miss Time's assault course, sniffing an idea here, a theory there, moving on, and nudging, one hopes, ever closer to the throne of doubt. Meanwhile I shall be on my knees in the cathedral, praying 'O Lord, let him stand for nothing lest he should believe it'. Not, of course, that I shall expect my prayer to be answered.

And that's my opinion.

The long slide to paradise

Like most good things, skiing costs a lot and serves no purpose.

If you believe in evolution then skiing suggests it's come to an end. Man no longer has to fight to survive. At the weekend he can afford time off from hunting and child rearing to don hundreds of dollars' worth of clothes, rent thousands of dollars' worth of equipment, and ride millions of dollars' worth of ski lift up the side of a mountain in order to slide down it.

But if you don't believe in evolution, if you believe that God made man in his own image, then one glance at the skifield and you get doubts. If these people dressed in puffer-fish jackets and wigwam hats are baby godlings then it suggests nasty things about the manufacturer of the universe, suggests indeed that earth is probably a cosmic joke, which of course it is. And skiing is part of the fun.

When I was a kid at school we made ice-slides by pouring water on the playground. Once they had frozen we ran at the ice, hit it at speed and slid with feet a shoulder's width apart and arms spread like wings, whooping and squealing all the way to the end of the ice. Then we fell over. But the five-second slide was a wonder. It was cheating the natural order of things; it was movement without effort. We felt like gods, like freewheeling kings of loco-motion, the albatrosses of solid earth, untameable lords of creation. Ice-sliding was the childhood equivalent of gin.

The other joy of ice-slides was that they were illegal. Teachers with gloves and moustaches banned them. Ice-sliding, said the teachers, was dangerous. We could break bones. What the teachers meant was that if they tried it, they would break bones. Their osteoporotic hips would shatter like chalk. We never broke bones. We skinned knees and banged heads and funny-boned elbows into numb agony but we were fine. We were the flexible gods. We had rubber bones, the bones of young chickens. The teachers banned the ice-slides for the same reason adults ban all children's activities – envy.

Adults like all children's games. Adults at parties drink gin, talk politics and think sex, but they would rather play sardines. In their hearts adults prefer *Hairy MacLary* to *Anna Karenina*. They prefer *The Simpsons* to the news. But guilt makes them want to attain some mythical status called adulthood. Adult-hood equals seriousness. It probably stems from having money.

Skiing, then, is the perfect adult pastime. It reverts to childhood but it costs a lot. The expense validates the exercise. It also validates the Pajero.

One annual trip up the ski-road justifies the rest of the year puttering from home to mall to school in a vehicle built of testosterone.

Because skiing is just ice-sliding made expensive, it is best done by children. Infants use skis as a dolphin uses flippers. Toss a newborn child on to a ski slope and it will start doing parallel turns. Toss a fully fledged adult on to a ski slope and it turns into a child who can't stand up. Adults use skis as a dolphin uses a can-opener.

Just as ski slopes come in degrees of difficulty, so skiers come in levels of incompetence. The level not to be at is adult-beginner level. Adults cherish dignity which they achieve by relinquishing all activities that look undignified. Dancing is one such activity. So is sex. So, *in excelsis*, is learning to ski.

For the adult beginner, putting one ski on is a breeze. Putting the second on is a farce. Like any farce it involves a lot of falling over. Unlike a farce it involves falling over in full view of thousands of brightly coloured children who ski past at a speed that resembles a noise.

To learn to stand up and slide, adults hire an instructor who doesn't speak English. Instructors who do speak English are working in Austria. This is part of a global plan to make ski lessons incomprehensible. The longer you remain at the toddler stage the more lessons you have to pay for.

Nevertheless the beginner eventually masters the snowplough. This means grinding down the bottom bit of the learner slope at a speed that resembles reverse. The correct physical posture for this exercise is that of a man squatting over a foreign lavatory. The correct facial expression is terror.

But once the terror leaves, the pleasure comes. The pleasure of sliding down slopes which the grooming machine has turned into alpine streets. The pleasure of speed, of innocent danger, of whooping to the frosted air, of trailing clouds of glory, of falling down and laughing and getting up and going again, of letting go of adulthood to snatch at the tantalizing tail of freedom, fun and folly. Like life itself it is pointless, expensive, downhill and glorious. Could you ask for more?

A tale of two mice

Time passes and things change. And I find it is always the little things that tell the story best, that toll the gap between then and now. Little things like mice.

I remember with sunlight clarity waking on a sofa twenty years ago with a regulation hangover. The sofa was vinyl, the pillow a stinking cushion, the blanket a stiff and dust-drenched rug and the house a dump.

We called that house *Beirut*. Friends rented it on the grim fringe of a huge city, amid streets where litter slapped the ankles and where children had shaved heads, feral eyes and mothers to whom chance had been cruel in every way and had scored its cruelty into their faces, their clothes, their body shapes.

But dawn reaches even such a suburb as this and even such a house as *Beirut*. It filtered down to this living room, this vinyl sofa, this rented temporariness and woke me. Unknown numbers slept upstairs, but I was alone below. The bladder was vocal, the throat scarified, the head like a stifled groan. Half awake I watched as the sun pierced the dirty windows, sidled across the room and lit a vast second-hand TV with an indoor aerial, a tubular chrome chair, a wrong-height table, and a mouse.

A mouse the same colour as the carpet. And I lay still to watch it. It was aware of my presence but not as a life form. I was furniture. I was terrain. It was alert but not nervous, a tiny suburban antelope on the carpet's Serengeti. I watched until the ache of the bladder became like the shriek of a saw on a nail and I had to get up. The mouse disappeared not when I moved, but at the exact moment when I decided that I would move.

By the time I had used someone else's toothbrush, drunk a pint of water and made an instant coffee (I was a hardened sleeper in other people's houses in those days and could find the coffee in any kitchen in the Western world) and returned to the vinyl and the rug, the day was dirtily under way and the mouse a memory, a dawn encounter that had felt like a strange privilege. A communion of sorts. Something tinily good. That, as I say, was twenty years ago.

The memory bubbled up last week because a woman sent me a mousetrap. She comes from Whangarei and the mousetrap from the United States. Kind Mrs Whangarei had heard me on the radio saying that I was battling mice.

I always know when there's a mouse in the house because the cat stares at the fridge. It can stare at the fridge for hours. Mice go behind the fridge because there they find house-crud. House-crud is hair and toenails, grease and crumbs. It gathers only in houses. You never come across house-crud in a forest. And while the mouse frolics in the crud

139

the cat sits attent with its tail wrapped around its base like a draught excluder.

Across the back of the fridge there's a sort of lattice. I can only guess at its purpose but to a mouse it's a climbing frame. During the night the mouse hillaries up the lattice and on to the roof of the world and finds bread and cheese. The bread's in a plastic bag, the cheese in a mousetrap. If the mouse goes for the bread it runs a slight risk of suffocation in the plastic bag. If it goes for the cheese it runs no risk at all. My mousetrap serves as a feeding station. The only mouse it ever killed was noticeably elderly and had the build of Buddha. I suspect it died of shock. Every other morning I have found a bare trap, ravaged bread, a dandruff of droppings and the cat still staring at the Kelvinator.

Until, that is, Mrs Whangarei sent me her dread engine. It is called The Better Mousetrap. I presume that the factory that makes this trap is easy to find because the world will have beaten a path to its door. The trap is made of grey plastic, admirably simple in design and as touchy as a feminist.

I baited it last night and went to bed. In the morning the cat was asleep on the sofa. On the floor a blob of mouse innards. On the fridge a triggered mousetrap. In the mousetrap a spread mouse. Its back-end looked like the ragged muzzle of a blunderbuss. Or like Beirut. The mouse had not had time to assume a look of surprise.

And it seems to me that these two stories, in their every detail, illustrate more clearly than anything else I could write, the gap between youth and middle age.

140

Across the grunting board

I've never seen a woman playing chess. Chess requires a peculiar form of intelligence and I don't know if women have it.

I do know that I don't. I play chess rarely and badly. I can see several moves ahead, but those moves are always my moves. Somehow I cannot see the game from both sides of the board at the same time. Many players have made me look foolish, but I have met three players who made me look imbecilic. Two of those players were men.

The third was a machine. It was a folding chess computer which I bought at Heathrow to while away a flight to Canada. I set the machine at cretin level. It thrashed me before we took off. But I persevered and during the flight a group of people gathered at my shoulder to watch my humiliation. Every time I made a move I heard them suck their breath through their teeth. On an aeroplane it is impossible to throw things out of the window so somewhere over the Arctic Circle I gave the computer to a Russian.

Russians like chess. If at any time the world champion is not a Russian he is from some adjacent and similarly vodka-sodden, gloom-laden, formerly communist country. I don't know why. The present world championship is being played between Alexander Kramchik and Gary Kasparov. Gary does not seem to me to be the most Russian of names, and indeed in the eighties Kasparov defied his communist masters, but Russian he is and very good at chess. The only time he has been beaten for the world title was in his 1997 rematch with Deep Blue. Deep Blue was a computer. It won, just, and was promptly dismantled.

I do not find it remarkable that Deep Blue won. Deep Blue could make twelve billion computations a second. What I do find remarkable is that Kasparov won several games.

Apart from Deep Blue, Americans don't seem to be much good at chess, although they did have a champion called Bobby Fischer. He played for, and I believe won, the world title some time in the seventies, which was the last time chess was sexy. The attraction of Fischer was that he was mad.

His apparent lunacy subtly confirmed the idea that chess is subversive. It is not an all-American activity like baseball or shopping. Even the vocabulary of chess suggests subversion. Instead of champions they have Grand Masters. Like the Ku Klux Klan.

I am in awe of chess. It is not just that the game is endlessly complex, nor that it is warfare by another name, but that it is so very human, so accurate a mirror of that animal called man and the societies that he forms. The truth lies in the pieces.

The king is a feeble thing, a mere totem. So bloated with power is the king that he can only shuffle a step at a time. He shelters behind his defensive wall and takes the first opportunity to scuttle to the corner of the board.

The castle is a loyal and honest piece that looks after its master as the Earl of Kent looked after King Lear. It moves in emphatic straight lines and when the battlefield is sparsely populated it can win a match in a few decisive strides. But when things are politically complex the castle is unwieldy and somehow stupid.

The bishop may lack the castle's death grip but it is a far smarter piece. Like the castle it is capable of sizzling attacks, but it's also a sleazy ecclesiastical sidewinder, less obvious, able to squeeze through crannies. Most devious of all is the knight. The knight dances strangely into corners and out again. Trapping a knight is like trying to swat a mosquito. Always it flits beyond reach then returns to tease you.

In front of them stand the pawns, the plodding foot soldiers, recruited from the working classes, serving a purpose but in themselves deeply undistinguished. Once the battle warms they can be tossed aside like used tissues. Their only virtue is their physical existence. Unlike every other piece they cannot go backwards. They walk stolidly to extinction. Their graves are not recorded nor their memories honoured.

I have known people like all of these pieces. But it is the queen who dominates the board. She can go anywhere and do anything while her hubby quakes at her back. Chess would appear to be the most feminist of games. So why is it that few if any women play it? Is it perhaps that over the centuries while the men have been grunting over the chessboard the women have been doing all the work? Is it? It might be so.

Soy science

Science is slow. The boys in the labs can take thousands of years to catch up with common people and common sense. For example since the days of the dinosaurs people seeking relief from the pain of piles have been toddling along to wise women to collect a distillation of rosemary or a comfrey poultice. But it has taken the test tube wallahs with their lab coats and outlandish sexual preferences several millennia to confirm by analysis what the piles sufferers and everyone else discovered years ago, which is that the medicinal value of these herbs is roughly nil.

And it's a similar story with soy sauce. One sniff of the stuff some thirty years ago was enough to tell me it was nasty, but only in the last week has science lumbered up like some sort of intellectual hippo and announced in its mangled English that, well, blow me down, I was right all along. And so now all the sycophants in the West who have fallen for propaganda about the wisdom of the East and who start each day with a joss stick and a mantra and a cup of soy have got something new to worry about. Which is all rather pleasing to us visionaries.

The East has been on the rise in the West since the sixties, when The Beatles – four Liverpudlian grease monkeys deified by a zillion pubescent female hormones – discovered that fame, wealth and a bit of a sing-song were not delivering happiness. So off they trundled in search of eastern enlightenment. The yogis and maharishis saw them coming a mile off, milked them for a fleet of pink Rolls Royces and sent them back West to carry on warbling.

But the little Beatles were merely dandruff in the wind of western trends. Once western spirituality had been flattened by the combined tsunami of science and shopping, a whole generation was left with nothing to believe in. The result was an eastbound procession of jeans-wearing, Joan Baez-humming sons and daughters of Californian dentists who picked over the pretty bits of ancient creeds in the hope of finding a sense of purpose and a lot of sex. It all ended in tears of course except for the entrepreneurs of everywhere East of Turkey who made stacks of money by selling the hippies drugs. You can see the sad remnants of this lost tribe of capitalism lingering skeletally from Goa to Mount Fuji, still finishing every sentence with 'man' while combing their shreds over their bald spots.

These people are jetsam now, stranded on the beach of yesterday's fad. Today's trendy seekers have returned to their native habitat, the shopping mall, and are hanging around in those extraordinary stores awash with incense and purple neon, buying runes, crystals, tantric tarot cards and origami condoms. None of this stuff works either, but it's probably got a few more years left in it before the next fad rumbles up to fill the abyss of meaninglessness.

Meanwhile the great soy scandal has made life even more difficult for the equally lost but more obedient many, the ones who read *Consumer* magazine, look for the ticks on tins and have nightmares about buying an electrical appliance which is suddenly recalled by the Taiwanese manufacturer on the grounds that if incorrectly installed it might wreak permanent damage on junior. Now that they're also obliged to read the list of ingredients on bottles of soy, the poor honeys will have even less time for looking at the sky and thinking, which of course is what got us all into this mess in the first place. Not that we did the thinking that actually wreaked the damage. That distinction goes to the bespectacled ones in lab coats, Newton, Darwin, Einstein and all the rest of them, whose rationalism blew the general public's age-old spiritual comforts into irrecoverable pieces.

It should be noted however that the sauce-testing boffins have overlooked one teensy wisp of evidence in their condemnation of soy, which is that the races who drink the stuff from nappy to shroud happen to be the longest-lived and least cancer-ridden races on the planet, but I doubt if anyone's going to let that get in the way of a good food scare.

Meanwhile none of this groping for hope helps the poor people with piles who are still toddling along to anyone who promises them even a hint of relief. A woman told me the other day that the best thing she knew for piles was a frozen tea bag. I asked her what property of tea it was that offered such balm and she said she suspected it was more the property of the frozenness and I said oh and thought it all rather neat though I couldn't help wondering and indeed worrying what happened as the tea bag thawed.

Diggers and dozers

Today I sought help from a man who loves what I hate.

I knew him first as a third former, his hands hidden up the sleeves of the jacket he was to grow into. Back then he called me, as was proper, sir.

I remember he built a contraption with two chutes for a fair at the school where he was a pupil and I a teacher. He sat at the top of the chutes with a bucket of eggs. He would roll eggs down each chute simultaneously. A punter who had paid a dollar stood below. And if the punter caught the eggs above his head he won a prize and if he missed he suffered. A crowd gathered and the dollars piled up. I was impressed by the ingenuity of the boy.

A year or two later I taught him English, or at least I issued him with books. He said, as was proper, thank you sir, but as I read bits from the books and made much of the sweetness of the prose or the clarity of the thought or the whatever of the whatever he said hum. He was always courteous and when I asked for essays he fought words onto the paper but all the while it was evident he was elsewhere. He wanted to be doing.

That's what classrooms are for, of course, to yoke the young together by the force of adult law and let them lick at other ways of being to see how they might taste. And then, when all's been done that can be done to let them know the world is various, they burst the bonds that held them there and go the way they choose. And if the way they choose is honest to the way they are they have a chance of happiness.

Today the boy who rolled the eggs is happy. He runs his own contracting company. He's got diggers and dozers and dirty boots. He makes decisions on the run, deals in tons of substrate, lorry loads of crusher dust and twirling tankers of concrete. Show him a piece of land and he can see the subdivision lurking there and he can make it happen. He likes the thrill of altering and building. He likes the challenge of the dealing doing world. I prefer books.

I rang him today because I'd like a house that backs against the bush but still remains in rolling distance of the pub and people. I think I may have found the piece of land to build it on and can almost see the Hansel and Gretel cottage I would like with space for dogs to run and chickens to scratch and far from any neighbours, for neighbours are like going back to school.

I called the contractor because I didn't know what to do next. I can read the relevant documents, can ring the people who can do the sort of stuff I need but I'm an innocent who shrinks from such affairs. I feel like a goldfish in a tank of sharks. I like to read and write and laugh but when it comes to building I'm a third former who knows he'll never grow into his jacket.

And so I rang him up and though he was busy doing this and that – a pipeline here, a new road there – somehow he found time to come round in the sort of truck I don't know how to drive and we went to the place where I would like to live. We got out of the truck and looked at the land with utterly different eyes and minds. I saw a semi-rural dream of silence. He saw gradients and sewage lines and where the slope would need retaining walls. But we both said it was nice.

He said what it would cost to build a road and where would be the place to build a bench, whatever that may be, and how a bit of cash could work particular wonders and what the local council would be likely to require and he made the whole thing seem not only possible but even straightforward. I gawped, still daunted, but also impressed in a way I doubt he ever was in my classroom.

Why it should be that what repels one man attracts another, why the gap between natures should sometimes be so wide that we can only gesture across it, I can't tell you. But I can tell you that I am glad that it is so, and I can also tell you two things that can span that gap: the undervalued virtue of courtesy and the greatly valued stuff called cash. I offered the man cash for his time. He wouldn't hear of it. And so instead I gave him, as in days gone by, a book. And he said, as was proper, thank you, Joe.

Beneath the visiting moon

I was Mark Antony but I wasn't supposed to know. When I arrived at the party the hostess clapped a little sticker on my back, told me that it identified me as an historical character, that I had to find out who I was by asking questions of other guests, but that no one was allowed to tell anyone else directly who they were. Why not, I asked, or more to the point, why? To break the ice, she said and laughed her delightful hostess laugh.

All of which was harmless of course, except that local rules dictated that you weren't allowed a drink until you found your character's historical partner.

Well, I've always loved a game so naturally I went straight to the bathroom, read the sticker in the mirror, found Cleopatra – whose appearance, it has to be said, suggested that whoever planned the party at least had a sense of humour – and led her to the bar. She came willingly. On the way we passed an attractivish twenty-five-year-old addressing a ninety-year-old Napoleon.

'I think I may be Josephine,' she said.

'What was that?' he said, fingering his hearing aid.

'I'm Josephine,' she shouted.

A light suffused his ancient face in a way that made you mentally rehearse the correct sequence for administering CPR.

'I'm very pleased to meet you,' he said.

'No, I don't think you understand. You're Napoleon.'

'What's that?'

Five minutes later Cleo and I had acquired satisfactory quantities of drink, discovered a fierce mutual lack of interest and separated, which was fine for her who had arrived with a crowd, but less fine for me who had arrived alone and now found myself in the company of Henry VIII who turned out to be a quantity surveyor whose manner was so inoffensive I found it offensive. He also refused to tell me what a quantity surveyor actually surveyed quantities of, on the grounds that he was not going to talk shop at a party. I like shop. The details of what people do interest me. The world is mundane, but other people's mundanities are at least different and more or less honest. Admittedly I didn't want to know about quantity surveying all that desperately but I did want to know about it more than I wanted to know about the quantity surveying viewpoint on All Black line-outs.

Oh, why do we do it? Why do we bother to pretend to be social? Is there anything more hateful than small talk? Youth is the time for parties, by which I probably mean that youth is the time for sex, or at least thinking about sex, or imagining that parties will lead to sex, which, by and large, they didn't, at least not for me, although the hope always lurked in the wings like a prodding stage manager, urging one towards the crowd.

Besides, when young, out was always better than in. Out meant possibilities. In meant flatmates and a sinkful of dishes. But these days, in is good. It's warm and quiet with dogs and books, while out is crammed with two-way boredom. But out I still go, driven by I don't know what, to functions.

And the things we have to do to make them work, these party things, these forced middle-aged social events. Fancy dress for a start. Have I the words to sing the horror of fancy dress parties? I'm as fond as the next man of pulling on high heels and a suspender belt, and I enjoy surprising taxi drivers, but after the first insincere ooh la la, Robin Hood remains a quantity surveyor and Maid Marian remains his schoolteacher wife with the bad veins, and in the end a long bow and a fringed jerkin don't prevent people discussing the All Blacks.

Little children don't need ice-breakers. They don't even need booze. Throw a kiddies' party and they just get right on down to eating and fighting in an admirably primitive exhibition of self.

What happened in the years between then and now is something like the cooling of the earth's crust. The outer skin thickens and solidifies. The magma's still there as hot and volatile as ever but it is contained, and drilling down to it is long slow work, work not to be achieved in an evening of snacks and frocks and games. It becomes less possible to forge an instant friendship. It seems less worthwhile to try.

And when the evening's done, the people who were part of it depart and sink back into their homes and ease off their shoes and wonder why they went, and are convinced like Cleopatra that there is nothing left remarkable beneath the visiting moon.

D-day was last Friday

I have destroyed a lot of living things. Over the course of forty-four years I must have eaten whole herds of animals, flocks of birds, shoals of fishes and several ounces of vegetables. I have swatted, squashed and poisoned innumerable insects. I have killed an abundance of plants by putting them in my garden. But now all that has changed. For the first time I have added to the stock of life. I have become a father. There wasn't much to it.

Two of my hens became broody. I put golf balls under them which seemed to satisfy them, but it didn't satisfy me. Driven by unfamiliar instincts, I acquired a dozen fertile eggs from the earth-mother of Gebbies Valley and swapped them for the golf balls. Hen One welcomed her eggs by trampling them to an omelette.

When I removed the omelette, Hen One moved in with Hen Two. Together they sat on the six remaining eggs, staring into nothingness, waiting, compelled by instinct, barely eating and drinking, the colour slowly seeping from their combs. When I intruded they pecked at me. Sometimes a third hen would pile into the same nesting box. I feared for the eggs.

Nevertheless I counted my chickens before they hatched and in the hope of plenty I built them a palace. It's got windows and weatherboards and a lot of four-inch nails and a door that sometimes opens easily and a choice of perches and a line of nesting boxes with room service. To join the palace to their present hovel I built a cat-proof, dog-proof, bomb-proof pen. My builder's mate was a television presenter without whose helpful suggestions I would have finished in half the time.

Eggs take twenty-one days to hatch. D-day was last Friday. I rose at dawn and took a flask of coffee and two dogs up the garden. Mid-morning I heard cheeping. A chick emerged from the nest to take its first look at the world. It copped a close-up of me and the dogs and retreated.

Four of the eggs came to nothing. The fifth hatched then died. The hens tossed the corpse from the nest, refused all offers of counselling and got on with tending to the living. So there's just the one chick, an only child with a doting father and two mothers. It will be spoiled rotten.

It has inherited its mothers' intelligence. This afternoon it tried to eat a nail. It has also inherited many of the features of its great-grandfather several billion times removed. For if you were to take my chick and shave it and lay it on a piece of paper and draw around it with a pencil, the outline on the paper would be the outline of a dinosaur, or at least the outline of one of those unconvincing mock-ups of dinosaurs that star on television. For though my chick is the size and texture of a tennis ball, it

157

carries itself like a dinosaur, it has the scaly feet and the blinkless eye of a dinosaur and like a dinosaur it sprang from an egg. It is evolution in the flesh.

But evolution looks forward as well as back. When I watch the chick and its mothers in their pen I am reminded of nothing so much as a toddlers' picnic. The chick scampers and wanders, but if the dogs come too close it scuttles back to its mothers, to bury itself in their skirts. The mothers' broops of alarm subside into a sort of purring, like human mothers at the park who have retrieved their children from the edge of the road.

Chicken education happens fast. In only three days the chick has gained weight and courage. It has learned to peck and scratch. Today it roams further than it did yesterday. In a few weeks it will be a teenager giving the fingers to the dogs. In three months it will be laying its own eggs – unless it turns out to be a rooster, in which case it will be mounting its mothers.

A month ago this chick was scattered atoms. Now it's got a ticking heart. It can see. It is tempting to call the birth a miracle. But it is the opposite of a miracle. It is ordinary and essential, the mundane reality of reproduction. The hens are not surprised by it. The dogs would like to eat it. Blind instinct is at work.

Why then, from the top of the evolutionary ladder, should I be the only one to coo over fluffy vulnerability? Me with my freezerful of chicken portions. I don't know and I'm not sure that I care.

Deep in the dogs

It's Christmas. Raise the drawbridge, drop the portcullis, nail the letterbox shut and draw the curtains. But it's no good. Christmas gets through. Only today an electronic Christmas card slid into my computer, starring a snowman and a sledge and a poem of greetings beside which Al Gore's concession speech seemed a model of sincerity.

The dogs and I flee daily to the hills for long meditative Scrooge-meets-Wordsworth walks. But then some fool in the pub tells me I shouldn't. Why, I say. Grass seeds, he says. Pfui, I say with emphasis on the f, but nevertheless I listen.

Apparently I'm endangering the dogs. Grass seeds can lodge between the pads of a dog's paw where all is dark and damp and composty and, having lodged there, they can sprout and wreak horrible damage. What sort of damage, I ask. Use your imagination, he says. Pfui, I say again, but while it's perfectly all right, indeed admirable, to say pfui to a bloke in the pub, you can't say pfui to the imagination. Well you can, but it's about as effective as saying 'stay' to my little black mongrel. Neither she nor my imagination ever attended

159

obedience classes. Give my imagination a horror scene to play with and it's like a ferret in a chicken coop.

And so the mind conjures images of grass seeds lodging in paws and sprouting and sending shoots up the inside of my dogs' legs. The shoots follow the paths of the veins, drawing sustenance from the marrow, silent and insidious, blindly driving up towards the light, until suddenly they burst alien-like from the dogs' backs. The dogs yelp with a suffering I can alleviate only with a mower.

But I have told my imagination to sit and though it has continued to whine I have ignored it. Up the hills once more go the dogs and I for the joy that is in them. The warm wet spring has done wonders for the grass. It is more than dog deep. The dogs bound through it like furry dolphins. When they stand still they disappear. Meanwhile I sneeze along behind them through the wake of pollen.

My dogs have both been fixed and so lead an enviable existence from which the main source of expense and misery has been excised by a scalpel. I wish someone would spay the grass. Its repro-ductive weaponry is formidable. There are seeds like spears, and seeds like arrow-heads, and sticky seeds, and seeds with hooks on and above all there are little bullet seeds with a pair of pointed ends. But the man in the pub was wrong about the seeds. The dogs are fine and dandy. It's me that is under attack. The seeds pierce my clothing, gather in trouser cuffs, stick in hair, mass in shoes and sink into socks. How they manage it I don't know but the bullet seeds in particular know how to burrow into socks like moles of malice. And, having burrowed, they scratch. They scratch wickedly and irresistibly. I weigh thirteen stone, and a seed weighs approximately nothing, but it brings me down. I sit, remove my shoe, remove my sock, remove the seed, replace the sock, replace the shoe, stand up and the seed's still there. When I get home I try washing the socks but seeds scoff at such feebleness. They're as persistent as Christmas.

And so it was yesterday that the seeds took me to Horrorville. Off to the shopping mall I drove where I found a convenient car park in little under an hour. Shunning the giant synthetic Christmas tree crowned with some sort of electrical bird that squawked as I passed, I sought out the shoe shop. I want, I said to the frazzled girl, a pair of shoes that are rugged enough to climb hills, that can be worn without socks and that do not collect grass seeds. She led me gently by the hand to a display of the sort of shoes that, in youth, one vowed never to buy. Ranged before me were a hundred pairs of the strappy brown sandals worn by chemists on holiday, disciples in nineteenth-century oil paintings and people who shouldn't wear shorts but do. 'There you go,' she said, 'Jesus boots.' I bought two pairs to run away from Christmas in.

Hope and pile cream

I have developed an allergy. I had suspected it for a while. Last night I conducted a clinical trial to settle the issue for good or ill. It turned out ill and so did I. I woke this morning stuffed with phlegm, filled a few handkerchiefs and headed for the pharmacy as soon as it opened. There for the usual amusing price I acquired a box of pills to add to the collection in my bathroom.

A bathroom is a beauty parlour and a doctor's surgery. Every bathroom cabinet contains only two types of stuff: things to make you sexy and things to make you well. If the well-making things exceed the sexy-making things the owner is over forty.

The only lockable room in the house, a bathroom is a place of confession where we strip away our disguises and the poor bare forked animal comes face to face with itself. The bathroom is a place of loving and loathing, a place of hope and pile cream. And the things that accrue in a bathroom tell a raw and honest biography of its owner.

As infants we have no need of pills or bathrooms. The world is a playpen and dirt is a friend. Our bodies are pliant as rubber and our teeth whiten themselves. Wounds heal while we watch. Then comes adolescence. Strange things happen to the body, self-consciousness becomes a tyrant and the bathroom saga begins.

A teenage girl needs a bathroom of her own. Acres of unguents are essential to her mating game. Ditto the boys with their aerosols and hair gels, all bought in the hope that beauty comes from the chemistry lab. Wrong of course. Beauty comes from being young. It is one of life's neater ironies that we realize this only when we aren't young.

The advertisers play on youthful insecurities, hooking the children as easily as summer mackerel. It's a very good thing. Making kids spend money on cosmetics they don't need not only trains them for a consumer society but also grants revenge to adults whom time has robbed of everything but commercial cunning.

Once the storm of adolescence has abated, the bathroom cabinet becomes a chronicle of the war with time. Women fill their cabinets with replenishing agents and anti-wrinkling cream; men with Steradent and toupees. And one by one, as the years tick by, the medicines arrive. And having arrived, they stay. Each tells the story of a skirmish with the ultimate enemy. They are battle trophies, or perhaps charms against recurrence, or just agents we think we can trust in the war we must lose.

In my own bathroom stand penicillin which once saved my tonsils, Cataflam which eased my back, and Mylanta which did battle with a curry and lost. There's also a packet of slippery elm. I cannot imagine why I have kept it. It recalls a long-distant Sunday of diarrhoea when the local pharmacist was closed and I dared not risk the journey into town. I went to the healthfood shop. I was a desperate man and though slippery elm did not sound like the right sort of stuff I was assured that it was. It wasn't. Emphatically.

And now my bathroom cabinet has gained another trophy, a packet of antihistamines to counter my new-found allergy. My only other allergies are to wasp stings and ironing. I discovered the wasp sting allergy when I was twenty. A wasp zapped my neck and by the time I reached hospital they had to widen the door to get me in. To counter the swelling the doctor pumped adrenalin directly into my veins. It felt like running out on to Eden Park before a hundred thousand fans who loved me. I have spent the last twenty years deliberately vexing wasps.

But my new allergy is less agreeable. Indeed it is cruel. Indeed, I suspect that the President of the Immortals is toying with me. You see, I have always felt that youth isn't everything and that there are consolations to ageing. Youth may be the time of love and poetry but it is also ignorance and acne. And though the medicines may proliferate in my bathroom cabinet and though stiffness may become a memory for everything except my joints, nevertheless there is much solace to the found in the years of decline. There's solace in siestas and silence, solace in sitting and watching, solace in not having to compete or pretend, solace in knowing and not fretting about my long catalogue of weaknesses, and an abundance of solace in the occasional glass of something bracing. But on this spring morning which is as pretty as youth, I discovered for sure and for ever that I am allergic to red wine.

Love forty

When I was seven I knew what I wanted to do when I grew up. I wanted to be a ballboy at Wimbledon. Every year I dreamed of an invitation to crouch attentive by the net. I could sense in my bones the feeling of scampering and scooping across the faultless turf. I would please the crowd with subtle demonstrations of individuality. The unparalleled accuracy with which I rolled balls to the fat boys standing at the back would draw comment from the commentators. You must appreciate that this wasn't hope and it wasn't ambition. It was, uniquely in my life, a sense of destiny.

Tennis flared only briefly every year. It was like a swallow. Into the sunlight and showers of summer it swooped, something half-glimpsed and exotic, and then it was off, away, to go and play in other climes for the rest of the year. But for the two weeks of its presence it gripped the country and did particularly strange things to little girls. They forsook their dreams of ponies and ballet, one of which they couldn't afford and the other of which they couldn't do, and bought tennis racquets. They chalked lines on walls and for a few weeks the street resounded to the boing of weakly hit balls.

Although the tennis itself meant little to me, something of the game seeped into the corners of my mind. What I remember best is the women's tennis. The girls who bought tennis racquets aspired to emulate the perennial British champion, Virginia Wade. The commentators called her plucky which meant that she lost, but what I remember most vividly is her knickers. Presumably to deny the viewer any hint of taut female buttock those knickers were frilled and flounced. They looked like puffer fish. Or like one of those lampshades made of rice paper.

I remember rather more of a Frenchwoman called Françoise Durr. The commentators called Miss Durr dainty. Her racquet seemed a little too heavy for her to carry in one hand and when she served she kicked up her little foot behind her. If you listened carefully you could hear that foot saying oooh la la. She didn't volley and she didn't smash and she didn't win. She was the last repository of what in those days was called femininity.

Players such as Mademoiselle Durr were swept from the courts by a breed of women who had no time for femininity. They leapt and grunted and won. Their leader was Billie Jean King. The Billie said it all. Billie Jean hit the ball so hard that Françoise Durr fell over.

There are two types of tennis: the professional game and the real game. You watch one but you play the other. The gulf between the two is the gulf between what we aspire to and what we achieve. The professional game consists of people playing tennis. The real game consists of people looking for balls.

The world is too wide for tennis. The balls go exploring, and the wire netting round public courts conspires to help them. It allows balls to pass through it but not people. That netting is rusted at the base and bent up in corners. Weeds nibble at it. It rusts. It sags. It is, I think, the world's saddest stuff.

The game of tennis depends on the serve. In the professional game it is the breaking of serve that wins matches. In the real game it is the holding of serve. In the real game, the first service thunders into the foot of the rotting net or else passes the opponent at shoulder height. The second service flops over the net like anaemia.

Ground strokes are slightly different. It is not difficult to keep the ball in play, nor is it difficult to hit it hard. But it is impossible to do both at the same time. To keep a rally going you have to play patsy.

The real game depends on honesty. You are expected to tell your opponent when his shot goes out. The professional game has never heard of honesty. Professionals have the morality and manners of sewer rats, so tennis is the most official-intensive of games. In addition to the match referee and the umpire in his kiddy's high chair, there's a mob of line judges roughly equal in number to the New Zealand armed forces. One of these people is a net cord judge. He pays attention to the service and then sits back in the sun to watch other people taking exercise. These days, net cord judging seems to be not so much a job as a vocation. If, that is, it is too late to be a ball boy.

How far away is the lizard?

I like getting older. It allows me to be crusty. I like being crusty. For example, I submit copy to newspapers containing such sentences as, 'The lizard stood two inches from my nose'. But when it appears in print the lizard has crept five centimetres away and no reader over the age of thirty-five has any idea whether the lizard was lounging on the horizon or close enough to kiss.

Or am I alone in having gained no grasp of metric distances? I still don't know, for instance, how far a kilometre is. I think of a kilometre as being over there a bit, not a long way away but sort of half to three-quarters of the distance to being a long way away. In fact I think of it as being half to three-quarters of a mile. And I do know how long a mile is. A mile is just enough distance to feel that you've had a good walk. A mile takes exactly a quarter of an hour to cover at a brisk pace, the pace of, say, an accountant leaving a clinic for sexually transmitted diseases.

We used to measure in yards and I still do. A yard is a stride. Blindfold me and I will pace you out a 22-yard cricket pitch to within a foot. A metre is a stride and a bit. Try to pace out a cricket pitch in metres and you'll strain your crotch.

How tall is a tall man? He is and always has been six foot tall. How long is a foot? The answer is obvious and it's got toes. How long is a metre? If I recall it is handily the distance travelled by light in a vacuum during 1/299,792,458 of a second. But I don't recall. I had to look it up.

I do better with metric weights. I know, for example, how many apples there are in a kilogram. There are three more apples than I want. What I want is a pound of apples. A pound sounds like a weight. A kilogram sounds like an exercise machine.

When the police tell me to be on the lookout for a man 1.83 metres tall and weighing eighty kilograms, I suspect everybody.

How much is a pint? It is the amount of beer I want at a time. How much is half a litre? It is a swindler's pint. How much is a litre? It is a glass of beer that can be easily raised by a forklift truck or a German barmaid.

How long is an inch? It is exactly the length of the top joint of my thumb. I measure short things in inches because I always carry a thumb. How long is a centimetre? It is exactly the length of maggot. I rarely carry a maggot. If I hear that something is thirty centimetres long I have to imagine a maggot train. Or else I turn the centimetres into inches by dividing by two and a half.

Fortunately I can divide by two and a half. And I can do it because I spent my infancy in classrooms where the sun beat through the high windows and lit squares on the walls, squares that stretched into rectangles as the afternoon lengthened, all unnoticed by me because I was working out the compound interest on a sum of twenty-one pounds, ten shillings and threepence halfpenny invested at 5½ per cent over seven years. I am not naturally given to arithmetic but such exercise gave me a mind that handles numbers with the ease of a gibbon in a gym.

And I loved the old money. It had substance. I loved its ancient quirks. Twelve pence to the shilling. Twenty shillings to the pound. Five pounds to the pub. The abbreviation for pounds, shillings and pence was LSD, a hallucinatory bit of notation based on Latin and taking the money back a couple of thousand years. Thomas Cook was paid in this money. And the old pound sign was all twirls and flourishes. To write it was to feel rich.

Metrication and decimalization are irreversible. Thirty years ago the authorities threw out a few thousand years of accreted history for two good reasons. One was that everyone else was doing it. This is a sound principle of behaviour that has always been popular with lemmings. In human society it has been used over the centuries to justify everything from genocide to flared trousers.

But the second reason was and is irrefutable. That reason was trade. If you retained gallons and pints and feet and inches and pounds and ounces, how could you hope to trade with the rest of a world that operated in metric terms? Why, any economy run on such ancient oddities would wither and perish, just as the economy of, say, the United States of America has done.

171

Ringing the world

I once rang Fidel Castro. It was at the fag end of a party, not a teenage party with snogging on the staircase, but a middle-aged party, with daggers in the Sauvignon. But now it was late and the few remaining party-goers were barely going at all. They slumped on sofas with the dregs of drinks.

To cheer things up, I offered to phone the world.

'Name someone,' I said, 'anyone you like, and I'll get them on the line in three calls.'

It's a good boast. I have made it several times. People swallow the hook.

'Go on,' I said, 'anyone at all, famous as you like.'

'Elvis,' said a woman.

'Castro,' said a man.

'Give me the phone,' I said.

International directory enquiries gave me the number of some governmental office in Havana. I rang it and asked for *el presidente*. He was not available. He was at his country residence. Amazingly they gave me the number.

Castro intrigues me. He's the coelacanth of the Caribbean, the beast who should be fossil. The

Berlin Wall has been made into souvenirs, the Kremlin has tottered and fallen like a shot elephant, but Castro goes on going on.

Castro no doubt sees himself as independent but he was merely a child of his time. The seasons of thought and feeling govern how we all grow and Castro flowered into power when all was communism and revolution. But having flowered and enjoyed flowering, Castro refused to wilt. He kept his combat fatigues and his ancient mariner beard and he stopped the political clock.

Castro's Cuba sits at the doorstep of America and reminds that country of otherness. America distrusts otherness. America tells us that Castro's bad because he doesn't let his people grow fat. He has banned them from the shopping mall of Western capitalism.

I have not been to Cuba so I don't know what I should think of Castro. I don't know if he runs a secret police. I don't know if he tortures his foes. I don't know if his people love him or fear him, though I suspect they do both. I am sure that someone will write to tell me what to think but I suspect that things are not as simple as they seem and that he's neither good nor bad.

But I do know that he's mad. The evidence came this week when Castro collapsed while giving a speech. He had been speaking for a mere two hours. Apparently there was an hour or two more to come.

Any politico who speaks for two hours is mad. Megalomania has maddened him. Power has distorted his picture. He thinks too well of himself. He is plump with hubris.

Castro was speaking outdoors to a crowd of I don't know who. While he stood and spoke they sat and fanned themselves. But then his voice crumpled like paper and he fell against the lectern. The cameras panned away but the people carried on staring. They were staring at Ozymandias.

My name is Ozymandias, king of kings.
Look on my works, ye mighty, and despair.

Castro's works are Cuba and his own status. But his audience would have seen that though his status is unassailable, his body is not. The enzymes of decay are busy in it. And suddenly those enzymes had made their first statement. We have been patient, said the enzymes, but look, we have been working. We will win. Bear with us. Prepare to lose thy leader.

It was a remarkable moment, a point of pivot. On a short clip of official film, pride met frailty, vanity said hello to the worms.

Castro will not go willingly or soon. He has so much to lose he dare not lose it. He is his office. And sure enough, within minutes of collapsing he was back on the podium intent on finishing the great bore. But his audience had seen a different finish. They had seen that for Castro, as for Ozymandias, the lone and level sands stretch far away.

When at that party I rang Castro's country residence I said I was a dignitary from *Nueva Zelandia* and that I would like to speak to the great revolutionary papa on a matter of some urgency.

The secretary told me to *esperar un momento* and in the crackling of the tinny international line I felt unwonted excitement.

For though I had often boasted that I could locate anyone in three phone calls, the best I had done was the switchboard of the hotel at which Sophia Loren was staying. And now I was about to speak to international power.

The secretary returned. She was sorry. The revolutionary leader was having a nap. It was, she said, a warm afternoon.

'*Gracias*,' I said, and left the great leader swinging gently in his hammock.

Is Sod a god?

Sod's Law is no law. Otherwise known as Murphy's Law or, and more poetically, the Law of Utmost Perversity, it decrees that if a door says pull you push it. The principle of Sod's Law is that the world has set its face against us. Well, it hasn't. The world is with us.

We notice when things go wrong but not when they go right. I have a car. I have driven it every day for five years but I have written about it only twice – once when its alternator perished and once when both my dogs threw up on the back seat. Days when the alternator alternated properly have passed without remark, as have the days when the dogs threw up out of the window.

I have never written about my stove. My stove has been even more faithful than my car. It has heated everything that I have asked it to heat and although much of that stuff has proved inedible it would be churlish to blame the stove. Then yesterday it blew up.

I was boiling a vat of stew for the dogs. Years ago I discovered that I had a reverse culinary gift: I could put four ingredients that I liked into a pot and cook something that I did not like. But with dog stew you can't go wrong. The dogs think I'm Escoffier. To make the stew fill a pot with things that dogs find edible – defined as anything non-metallic – and boil them for a long time with rice. It smells filthy but it's foolproof fun.

Yesterday my stew looked like primeval soup. To thicken it I tipped in flour. It formed a crust on the surface through which the soup seeped and bubbled. I stayed to observe. It was like watching the birth of life. Spurts of gravy burst through the crust like magma. To hasten evolution I turned up the heat. Then the phone rang. And it was while I was talking to a friend about depression that the stove blew up. Prompted, I suspect, by primeval soup dripping into its electrical bits, the stove gave off a bang and a shower of sparks and died on the instant. I was annoyed, the dogs excited and the cat has yet to come back.

And so Sod's Law is invoked, I hate my stove and a story is born. For stories require adversity. People complain that the newspaper is full of bad news, but news by definition is bad. Unless something goes wrong there is no story. That is perhaps the difference between journalism and poetry. Journalism reports on things that go wrong. Poetry reports on things as they usually are. Journalism is more fun; poetry more true.

And now it is morning and I am waiting for the stove repair man and the air is so springlike and sweet that I would be declaiming to the hills Laurie Lee's 'April Rise' – 'If ever I saw blessing in the air'

– if the neighbour hadn't decided to call in a concrete cutter. The concrete cutter arrived with the dawn and a lot of equipment.

I have had few dealings with concrete cutters and I am uncertain exactly what it is that they do, although a little voice whispers that it is just possible that they cut concrete. If so, it's a trade like journalism in that it depends on something going wrong, on people laying concrete where they don't want it.

The concrete cutter manoeuvred his van with remarkable skill until he was satisfied that he had blocked all possible vehicle access to my house and then he set about making noise. He warmed up by placing speakers on the bonnet of his van and playing the sort of pop music that offends me, by which I mean music that is vacuous, tuneless, primitive, mendacious, aggressive and wrong, by which I mean all pop music apart from the few bits I like. Then he put ear muffs on. Finally he set to work with a saw and a road drill in a successful bid to recreate the soundtrack from *Psycho*.

I hate noise. I have always hated noise. It makes my brain clench. Instantly I have forgotten all the sweet mornings, all the long good days of silence. I feel at odds with the world and at such times it is hard but important to recall that Sod is only a minor god. His periods of sway may be memorable but they are also few. In time the stove man will come and the concrete cutter will go and if I were wise I would just lie down like a dog and wait for the good bits to happen once more.

It's a bit like cricket

The pornography of my childhood was a weekly magazine called *Angling Times*. I salivated over its black and white pictures of cod.

Last week I spoke on the radio about my fondness for fishing. Several people have since asked me how I could condone it. I don't know if I can. But I suspect that fishing is like cricket – either you love it or you are bewildered by it.

I am sentimental about animals but fish don't count. They're dumb, limbless and bald. On the evolutionary ladder they're one rung above mud. The rudest thing that Robert Graves could find to say about fish was that they were fish. Nevertheless I find them beautiful. Aquariums lure me and I stand for long minutes in front of fishmongers' slabs.

I have never been a fanatic but my brother was. Some people have a nose for fish and my brother could find them in a puddle. Living in England we fished in sluggish rivers and ponds the colour of tea for roach and rudd and bream and tench and chub and dace and perch, but I caught mainly gudgeon. The biggest gudgeon in history weighed in at just over four ounces.

We fished for pike as well. Pike are freshwater sharks. In my creel I carried a pike gag, a spring-loaded device designed to hold a pike's jaws apart while you rootle among its teeth for the hook. To my relief I never caught a pike, but one famous day my brother had his picture in *Angling Times* holding an 18-pounder by the gills. Behind him in the picture stood a tree. Behind the tree stood his little brother.

In the winter we spent freezing days on a wind-rattled pier tossing lead and lugworms into swelling grey water in pursuit of ling, whiting and flounders the size of playing cards. Once I saw a boy hook a conger eel. Everyone on the pier gathered to watch the fight. Despite its size, the fish was inert. When it broke the surface it showed a face of stupid grey malice. From its teeth dangled a beard of broken fishing lines attached to hooks embedded in its cheeks and palate. Excited men lowered a dropnet to haul it up. The fish saw the net, shook off its lethargy, snapped the line like cotton and sank back into the hospitable sea.

Why does all this excite me? It's hard to say but it's something primitive. I am in danger of coming over all mystical and Hemingwayesque, but water is a hostile element where the fish is at home. To bring it from the water is to assert dominion over it. To put it back is to assert even more.

Everything about fishing is right. The tackle is right. To me a tackle shop is like a jeweller's. I relish the engineered artifice of rods and reels and floats and hooks and flies. Being by water is right. Water makes good noises and is infinitely various. Any stretch of water is a parcel of puzzles and promises. No fisherman can cross a bridge without leaning over the edge and fishing with his mind.

Fishing gives rise to stories. On a foggy harbour in British Columbia I saw a fisherman in an inflatable dinghy hook a small salmon. A seal then took the salmon, and towed the man and his dinghy out of the harbour and into the fog, screaming. In Acapulco with a family-size hangover I briefly held a rod with a 300-pound marlin on the end. The fish tore off a screaming 100 yards of line, then dived and was gone. But it wasn't until I saw a friend casting a dry fly to trout on the edges of Lake Benmore in the Mackenzie Country that I discovered the best of all fishing. The dry fly may not be the most efficient way to catch fish but it is the most elegant, the most subtle and the most primal. I haven't the space and I probably haven't the words to explain its glories.

I flyfish poorly. I have fished for half an hour in the darkness, casting to fish that I could hear rising and all the while my fly has been stuck in my hat. I have caught any number of logs, branches, bushes and fences, and once, on the backcast, a cow. I have hurled countless flies at fish-shaped stones and bits of weed. But when last week, for the first time in over a year, I dropped a black gnat over a feeding trout and watched the fish nose towards it, rise with easy elegance, flash the white of its mouth and suck the fly in with an audible gulp, then I knew a joy that is rare, fierce and good.

Let it all hang out

Everyone knows that it is wrong to repress feelings. We must express them. If we don't they go bad and we go mad.

A popular forum for expressing feelings is television and in particular those afternoon talk shows, of which the most famous is the Jerry Springer show. There will be a Jerry Springer show this week. I do not know if its subject will be 'My wife left me for a dyslexic lesbian', or 'My son became an alcoholic at elementary school', but I do know who won't be watching it. Nancy Campbell Panitz won't be watching it. She's dead.

Nancy Campbell Panitz appeared on the Jerry Springer show, as did the person who allegedly killed her. He is Ralf Panitz her former husband. On the show he accused Nancy of stalking him, told her she was fat and unwanted and, by his own admission, sought to humiliate her. It worked. Apparently Nancy Campbell Panitz left the stage humiliated. Now, thanks to multiple stab wounds she has left an altogether bigger stage.

Jerry Springer has denied responsibility. 'I'm responsible for my show,' he says, 'and I love doing it,' but he insists that other people's lives are their own concern and in one way, of course, he is right. Jerry Springer did not stab Mrs Campbell Panitz.

His show and others like it are built on conflict. People with strong feelings are invited to express those feelings in front of a camera. The participants scrap. They start with words and sometimes they move on to fists and fingernails. The host is appalled of course, appalled by the violence, appalled by the overspill of emotion, appalled by the ballooning ratings, appalled by his pay cheque the size of the national debt of New Zealand.

I do not know if the people who appear on the Jerry Springer Show are paid, but I do know that they appear willingly. It is their moment of fame. And the petty hatreds and bitternesses and jealousies and rages that have preoccupied them suddenly gain the importance that their owners have always felt they deserved. In front of the cameras the little anonymous people become big important people with big important feelings. They fan the flames of those feelings and the more they fan them the more they please Mr Springer and they become excited by the unaccustomed feeling of being seen and noticed and of people taking an interest in them, and they strive to please the crowd and they discover that the more excited they become the more excited the crowd becomes and their feelings swell to block the sun.

I have no doubt that Mr Springer would argue that the feelings expressed on his show are real feelings felt by real people and that by providing a forum for the people to say what they feel he is doing them a service.

Well, I don't think Mr Springer has done Nancy Campbell Panitz much of a service, but more importantly I do not think the argument is right.

That argument assumes that it is better to express feelings than to repress them. It assumes that there is no third way. But there is a third way. It is the way that distinguishes adults from children.

Little children are slaves to feelings but adults are not. Adults can master feelings. They can recognize them and acknowledge them and come to terms with them. It is not easy but they can see that there is no profit in endless jealousy or anger. They can see that emotions can poison a life and by an act of will they can hold those emotions in check and wait for them to subside as they always do in the end. Then the scab forms and if the adult resists the urge to scratch it he is eventually left with a scar. Scars are not pretty things, but they don't kill.

But Jerry Springer is not interested in turning wounds into scars. He earns his money by ripping the scabs off wounds so that we can all enjoy the bleeding. And in the end the wretched story of Jerry Springer and Nancy Campbell Panitz reminds me of nothing so much as the story of Iago and Othello.

Iago's greatest delight was to manipulate emotion. He fostered Othello's jealousy, fanned it, fed it, breathed such life into it that it became 'the green-eyed monster which doth mock the meat it feeds on'. Maddened by that jealousy Othello kills his innocent wife, and then when he discovers his

184

mistake he kills himself. Iago laughs, the play ends, and the actors, having shown the consequences of ungoverned emotion, rise to go about their normal lives once more as Nancy Campbell Panitz never will.

Iago would have made a splendid talk show host. He would, indeed, have loved it.

Mind the gap

Six o'clock on the morning of Monday, March the
13th and I am at Heathrow airport leaning against
Terminal 3 and watching the sky over the car park
slide from black to grey. It is the first English dawn
I have seen for almost a decade.

Buses pull up in a shudder of diesel and disgorge
a stream of airport workers in coats and gloves and
with the remnants of sleep on their faces. I catch
snatches of ordinary conversations from lives that
have run on unthinkably for the years of my
absence.

I take the tube to town. My carriage is empty. In
the half-light of the morning the train passes street
after street of cramped two-storeyed houses, all
built of that unique London brick which is more
yellow than brown. Years of air have turned the
mortar black. Gardens lie dank and small, strung
with sagging clotheslines and littered with plastic
toys. Tight up against the windows of the train the
walls are covered in graffiti done by youths who
scaled razor wire to spray their elaborate coded
signs, marking their territory and their manhood
like pissing dogs.

The first passenger to board my carriage is a giant in building site boots. He wears a Swanndri and an All Black beanie hat, reads the sports pages of the *Sun* and drinks a litre of blackcurrant juice. As the train nears London and dives underground it gathers its freight of workers, men and women with their bodies wrapped against the cold and faces set against the journey. It seems that all the races of the world are represented in my carriage. None speak. Most read newspapers. An Indian girl curls around a book and draws her knees about her as if in front of the fire at home, buried in the famous isolation of the tube. At every station a recorded voice warns passengers to mind the gap.

When I stand to offer my seat to a middle-aged woman, other passengers look up in faint surprise. At Holborn I mind the gap and then allow escalators to haul me and my luggage up into the air. Popped suddenly into the city I stand to stare, forming a little island around which the people flow. City buildings of grey Edwardian stone, unremarkable but imposing and solid with sash windows and pediments and pigeons.

I ditch my luggage at an office, place my New Zealand bank card in a machine and am magically given money, then I idle down a side street to a tiny London park enclosed by wrought-iron railings painted black. The traffic noise has subsided to a hum. A squirrel scampers across the lawn, its tail plumed, its spine undulating as it runs. It stops, sits up like a typist, then sets off in a fresh direction. Pigeons bustle with their guardsmen's chests, purring and dingy, pecking at invisible scraps, lowering their heads towards each other like feathered bulls. Men and women with gloves and briefcases stride past my bench and do not look at me. When I crush a cigarette beneath my shoe, a pigeon inspects and rejects it, then a shambling man in a flying hat and a filthy parka picks it up. He has sores on his face. He looks about twenty-two.

No sun, but the light is softer and the air thicker than in New Zealand. I recognize it as the air, the light I was reared in, find most natural. Though by now I have spent as long abroad as I have in the country of my birth, I shall never know a place as I know this place. Its air and light and people, its countryside, cities and buildings are the yardsticks of my head. Each of us is calibrated by the place where we are reared. There is nothing we can do to erase the calibrations.

With time in hand I return to Holborn, let the tide carry me down the street at the brisk pace of people with work to go to. Holborn ends at Bush House, one of the homes of the BBC. The curved grey façade of the building is as impassive and formal and understated as a World Service newsreader.

Near here in the late seventies I laboured on a building site, drilling holes in floor joists, steering wheelbarrows along planks to tip rubble into skips and drinking Guinness at lunchtime. In a month or so we turned an elegant three-storeyed house into inelegant offices. I try to find the building but fail.

In the newsagents on the corner of Drury Lane the choice of newspapers is too rich. While I dither

188

five people buy papers. I find myself listening to accents and registering the subtle distinctions of class.

In a café beside a pub where Nell Gwynne is supposed to have drunk, I flick through *The Times* but find that the stories make no sense. I do not recognize the names of the politicians or of the footballers. Years have broken all the threads. The immediate world holds more interest. I listen to an argument between the sour woman who made my coffee and a delivery man with a box of croissants she doesn't want. Everything is vivid.

Turning a corner outside the café I am surprised by Covent Garden. Central London is like that. Though the city houses some 12 million people and its suburbs stretch for ever, most of its monuments and celebrated sites huddle in an area little bigger than central Christchurch. Round Covent Garden in the days of hair and freedom I must have spent a hundred riotous evenings with friends who had gone to the city to make money. Memories sweetened by time wash over me and I am chuckling in the street.

The phonebox smells reassuringly of vomit. Adverts for prostitutes cover the walls. Flicking through an address book stuffed with the telephone numbers of people I once knew, I find myself hesitating, not knowing where first to sink the spade into the past. I have a month in this country. As I dial the number of an old friend, my fingers are edgily nervous. A recording tells me the number is no longer in service.

Let's do dinner

Do you know him? His e-mail address is lesjones@uole.com, so I presume that he is American and that his name is Les Jones. If you do know him, do me a favour. Kick him. Kick him square in what Parisians called centre-ville. And when he is jack-knifed by that exquisite pain which takes a second or two to arrive but which, when it does arrive, brings a wave of throat-catching nausea before subsiding oh so slowly into draining universal grief, remember to take a photo. Send me the photo and I'll take you out to dinner.

We'll blow up the photo of the agonized Les and have it mounted on the restaurant table or, better still, we'll use it as the paper on which the menu is printed, a menu of the richest and finest foods that taste of self-righteousness and duty done and vice conquered and virtue rewarded. You will see no bill. I shall settle the bill. But I shall not be surprised if the Big Cheese himself looks down from his cotton wool palace in the sky and reaches out and tells me with a simple kindly sweeping gesture of the hand to put my credit card away. This one, says the Big Cheese, is on me.

If you don't know lesjones@uole.com but still fancy the celestial dinner, feel free to go hunt him. Perhaps you could use e-mail to lure him from his lair to meet you in some alleyway where all is dark and doubtful and your kicking boot is not immediately evident. Then swing it with a whoop and a skirl.

Harsh? What do you mean, harsh? You have gone mad. Your brain has been curdled by the hand-wringing pacifist folly of the late twentieth century. Grow up and grow strong. Get kicking.

For Les Jones, you see, persists in e-mailing me against my wishes. Les, whom I have never met, Les, who bought, I presume, my e-mail address from some perfidious organisation, has been trying to sell me stuff. Les calls this stuff GH. GH will make me feel ten to twenty years younger, says Les. GH will increase my energy levels by 84 per cent. GH will increase my sexual potency by 75 per cent. I have written back to Les. I have told him, with an irony that will have soared above his hardened skull, that 75 per cent of nothing remains nothing – for which relief much thanks, but that is by the by. More pertinently, I have gone on to ask Les in honeyed language to send me no more of his mountebank nonsense. I have told him that the only further correspondence I want from him is the name of the person from whom he got my address so that I can sue the traitor to hell and beyond. But Les has complied with neither request.

Of course Les Jones could be a nom de plume behind which the charlatans take cover to avoid the righteous swords of such as me. Or then again I suppose Les Jones could be *les Jones*, French and plural, as in *les filles de joie*, those demoiselles of the demi-monde who'll have you down the clinic before you can say *bonjour*. There could be hundreds *des Jones*, all with faces like skulls and too much make-up. Well, if so, let's kick the lot.

For the tables are about to turn. I shall be e-mailing Les from noon to midnight. I also have his fax number and I intend to clog it. I shall urge friends to do likewise. Because Les is a conster and a fraud and an intruder. He showers me with lies. He tells me that his oral spray of GH will increase my muscle strength by 88 per cent while reducing my body fat by 72 per cent and my hard-earned wrinkles by 51 per cent.

Go tell it to the birds, Les, because I have heard it all before. And so has everyone. From the wide-eyed Chaucerian peasant who gawped at the fairground spiel-maker with his patter and his bottle of dragon blood, to the dupe who lounges before the infomercials with a credit card and a telephone and a cavity where his mind should be. The only difference, of course, is that the peasants and the dupes of the long, gullible centuries have always been free to move away, to turn off the telly, to throw fruit or abuse at the charlatan. But I am not. Les Jones has me pinned by e-mail but he offers me nothing to twist or throttle. I can neither flee his rhetoric nor grab his jugular. His only exposed flesh is lesjones@uole.com and I am going hunting.

Love for lunch

Today I had lunch with a psychiatrist. This is not a behavioural pattern that I have previously exhibited – partly because I have known no psychiatrists but also because I have not thought well of their trade.

In twenty years of teaching I saw a number of disturbed children packed off to the couch. It rarely seemed to do them much good. In general I found that if anything mended the kids it was time and if nothing did then it was the legal system. My impression has always been that the brain is a dark, mysterious ocean and a large one, and that psychiatry is a blind fisherman in a very small boat.

Nevertheless this particular psychiatrist proved lively company at a party and we agreed to meet today in one of the more fashionable bits of downtown Christchurch. As I waited for her I sipped my beer and watched the crowd shuffling past in the winter sunshine. Perhaps it was the effect of my lunch-to-come but rather a lot of them looked mad.

The psychiatrist arrived fifteen minutes late, smiled like the sun, sat and did not apologise. I silently admired the ploy. We ordered Gewürzt-raminer and a dish of bits of fish.

The conversation soared. We discussed medita-tion, Sanskrit vowels, chaos theory, sixteenth-century philosophy, twentieth-century philosophy, the growing prevalence of depression, the nature of joy, the popularity and value of Prozac and whether bacteria could be happy, all with a formidable sweep of lightly-held knowledge to which I contributed several ums. I also refilled her glass twice.

And then we got onto love. Now I know a bit about love, and I said so. On the inside of my locker at school I had a photograph of Geoff Boycott. There was something about the way he held his bat, something about the sweet stretch of flannel over thigh pad that sang to my fourteen-year-old soul.

The psychiatrist looked quizzically at me over a slice of blackened monkfish, but I persevered.

And then, I said, over the horizon came puberty, marching strongly and letting nothing obstruct it. And with it came love.

She asked me to describe the symptoms of love.

Moping, I said, featured prominently, along with self-pity, grinding despair, sulking, moonlit vigils and a curious addiction to reading and writing poetry. Would she like to hear some?

Despite the monkfish she shook her head with some vigour, reached for a prawn and asked if I still suffered these symptoms.

With a tolerant smile I explained that I had grown beyond such emotional intensity and had indeed been free of the effects of love for at least two years.

The prawn went south, pursued by a swig of Gewürzt. 'And you call this love?' she asked.

I asked her what she would call it. She told me. There were several phrases. The least offensive was preoccupational emotive attachment.

Oh, I said, and I meant it to sting, but she swept on.

She acknowledged that to some extent psychiatrists were indeed fishing blind in a dark ocean, but there were some well-lit bits. You could, for example, dose people up with something mildly radioactive in the bloodstream, then get them to think certain types of thoughts and with the help of a machine study the bits of the head that were being used to think these thoughts. Every sense impression, she said, every feeling, every thought in the end is just a chemical reaction in the head, an influx of serotonin across the synaptic cavity or whatever. Now, she said, it was a curious coincidence but a colleague of hers was studying the sort of infatuation I had described. And her colleague had found a drug which seemed to cure it. The stuff was called – and I wrote this down to get it right – Trifluoroperazine.

She paused for effect and a morsel of snapper.

I said that I thought they should put Trifluoroperazine in the water supply. It would have spared us, for example, Donny Osmond or Boyzone. With Trifluoroperazine the Beatles today would be dodgy mechanics in a Liverpool backstreet, Tom Jones would be buying his own underwear, Winston Peters wouldn't get a single blue-rinse vote, Lady Chatterley could have got some knitting done, *Death in Venice* would have had a happy ending, someone would have punched Leonardo di Caprio and Lolita could have got School Cert.

'Yes indeed,' said the psychiatrist, and left me with the bill. It was $60.

Punching Prescott, he's my man

He's fat and I'd vote for him. I'd vote for him because he throws a left hand like a cobra's kiss.

Surely you saw it. Up stole the prole in his nasty shirt, his gut no doubt all lepidopterous but in his hand an emblem of his anger, a brittle bomb of reproductive juices, the simplest miracle in the self-replicating universe, an egg. And he biffed the egg. From a yard away. Smack into the wide political face of Mr John Prescott.

Mr Prescott is a man of importance and as befits a man of importance in this thrilling century he was ringed by a bevy of big-boys with walkie-talkies and framed degrees in jujitsu and feng shui, men with shoulders and suspicious eyes and a terrible sense of their own skill at hurting people, men whose every movement says, Come on sonny, try me.

Bodyguards long for the chance to toss President This or Prime Minister That to the ground and block the bullets with their own sweaty frames, as if to say, well, buddy, the world may recognize you and call you powerful but we are the ones who know what power is. Power is a knife or gun attached to rage or lunacy. And when feelings become missiles, we, the large and silent ones, will leap from the shadows of anonymity and become the men who matter.

Poor little big men thwarted by docility. All day their ears are assailed only by words, those Barbie doll weapons that break no bones. Words are thin stuff, the watery gravy of debate. The bodyguards yearn for a meaty stick or stone. It comes so rarely, that chance to take over, to smother and wrestle the frail important figure into the waiting limo and away to hospital or oval office.

And then, when it does come, whoa, they prove impotent. For all their glancing and dispassionate smile-free faces, for all their tall rectangularity, the surprise comes always as, well, a surprise. The bullet or the egg sings and security yelps into instant frenzy but it's too late. The blood or albumen's already dripping. The Pope is plugged. The President bleeds. The minister is egged. The deed is done, and their job isn't.

Not even the reverential cooing of small boys who are excited by the sense of weaponry can compensate for that deep knowledge of impotence. Security can do nothing. It might as well snooze long afternoons on the porch with a cup of hot dreams.

And how his bodyguards must hate Mr Prescott. For when at last the egg came whistling, from all of a yard away – oh the grand plans of detection and prevention, the minesweepers and sniffer dogs, the hovering choppers, the paraphernalia of surveillance, so manly, my dear, so impressively expensive, and so utterly ineffectual – when, as I say, that egg took wing, the big men missed it, missed it completely.

And furthermore, and how demeaning, they had their job usurped by the man they were there to protect. Fat Mr Prescott, all raincoat and rhetoric, did it himself. Somewhere between Mr Prescott's panting ventricles and his outsize underpants, something flicked like a lizard's tongue, something nameless and primal and as sharp as wit, and instead of flopping into incapacity as he was meant to do, he flung the fist. Out it flew as straight as virtue and caught the bloke a beauty on the jaw.

And wasn't it lovely. For everyone, that is, except the egg-thrower, the purveyor of surprise who was himself surprised, and for the bodyguards who had woken that morning in their xxxxos pyjamas and prayed for just this egg and just this chance to strut on telly. And also, of course, for the anger-management and anti-violence bods and all those others who abhor and deplore, and are shocked and disgusted. They have since abhorred and deplored and been shocked and disgusted in capital letters.

But they are wrong. The punch was lovely. That noise you heard when it landed was the sound of a million citizens ticking their ballot papers. For out of Mr Prescott's seeming lardiness came something people love and it is called righteous anger. This was suddenly not Mr Prescott, deputy prime minister, remote as parliament and polysyllables, but something altogether simpler and better. Who cares about the other stuff? Who cares if he talks of implementing policy initiatives? That's just the wittering of the necessary awful trade he practises. The punch was something else.

For one bright moment we saw Mr Prescott plain and we thrilled to what we saw. Or at least I did. I, who in Mr Prescott's shoes would have cowered and shrivelled, I found that punch funny and I found it just and I found it good.

Hobbes at the trough

It was Thomas Hobbes who said that human behaviour was dictated by two opposite and more or less equal forces, one being fear and the other desire. Hobbes would have been intrigued by smorgasbords.

Smorgasbords were unheard of in my youth. The nearest we came was in books and films where the higher classes had breakfast buffets featuring silver chafing dishes like plump partridges under which lay eggs benedict and kedgeree. I didn't know what either of these were, but they came with servants and tennis on the lawn and horses and girls in muslin and were out of my league.

But the inventions of the upper class have a habit of filtering down through the ranks in debased form. Hence the smorgasbord. It appeared, I think, in the late seventies as a successor to the fondue which was as fine a way as any yet invented of inducing people to buy equipment for buggering food about. The closest modern rival is the barbecue.

Anyway, the smorgasbord seemed the gastronomic equivalent of a round-the-world air ticket with unlimited stopovers. You could live at a smorgasbord. It was consumerism rampant. 'All You Can Eat' is probably the best slogan any ad man ever concocted. Hobbes would have been impressed.

The word smorgasbord sounds like a hog with its snout in something viscous but, in the original Swedish, smorgasbord is simply a verb meaning to economize on waiters while giving an illusion of opulence.

The essence of a smorgasbord is con food. Con food is placed at the near end. It aims to fill you up before you get to the good stuff. Soup is the original and still the best con food, although it has been challenged in recent years by salad. Salad used to mean leaves but with the arrival of the smorgasbord it has broadened its repertoire. Now there's an array of bowls containing what appear at best to be leftovers and at worst jokes.

Cold pasta like the flesh of the dead, only stickier; rice and sultanas dotted with sweetcorn and microscopic shrimps; tomato, cucumber, olives and cubes of polystyrene cheese soused in the sort of oil that is supposed to do your heart good and turn you into a wrinkled centenarian Italian peasant.

Beside the salads stand hot trays of cheap vegetables and lumps buried in sauce. One of these is a chicken dish and another a fish dish – indistinguishable to the eye and, as it later proves, to the palate – but one of them is also dangerously vegetarian. There's bread too and a bowl of boiled eggs cut in half and something moulded with beetroot and gelatin and a mound of traditional salad, which means very dark lettuce and very pale tomato. The tomato tastes of water; the lettuce of bitter water.

All this stuff should be shunned. That it isn't is testimony to Hobbes. Desire dictates that, on the bird-in-the-hand principle, the food in front of you, regardless of its merits, is hard to resist. Meanwhile fear warns you of the possibility of arriving at the end of the smorgasbord with too little on your plate. So on it all goes: spuds, a dab of chicken stew, a disintegrating smidgin of fish, Greek cheese, something green to assuage guilt, giant brine-soaked mussels with frill string round them like toothless gums, a dollop of unidentified gunk and then the slow shuffle while the sod in front of you picks the shrimps out of the rice salad and everyone looks at everyone else's plate.

Finally you reach a perspiring chef wearing an alarmingly stained apron and a hat like a fluted Greek column. In front of him sit two recognizable hunks of flesh under a theatrical spotlight. This concluding flourish is designed to give the belated impression of a medieval spit roast, a feast and celebration, all bounty and beneficence. Ham or beef, he asks. Your plate is a tumulus of ill-assorted substances. Nothing goes with anything. The choice of meat is irrelevant. Desire to eat and fear of missing out have rendered the meal a disappointment before you start. The promise of everything has become the delivery of too much.

The chef bloke balances too little ham on top of

your mound. It looks like a garnish. For a brief Oliver Twisty moment you keep holding your plate out, but the plate is full to the point of super-abundance, you don't want to look greedy and besides the chef has turned his attention to the next victim. Trailing morsels of salad you bear your plate to your table. It is impossible to know where to start eating this heap. You stab the ham and the spuds scatter and everything squashes into everything else and Hobbes chuckles.

Rein and bottle

God knows what I was doing there, and so do I. I know exactly what I was doing there. I was being bored, bored till my skull bubbled.

Across the detritus of a dinner table, the crumpled napery, the rinds of cheeses, the hardening shards of bread and the heel-ends of wine, I had tossed some idle and perhaps mildly disparaging remark about new-age sensitivities and suddenly I found myself being addressed by an unacceptable man. His clothes were unacceptable, his voice was unacceptable and his beard was, well, small nations have gone to war over less.

I seemed, inadvertently, to have broached the man's pet subject. It was not a subject which he discussed; it was a topic on which he lectured. And now he was lecturing me. His subject was emotion, and in particular the supremacy of emotion in our frail existences. Emotion is all, he said – or at least he would have said if he had ever acquired the knack of using words of fewer than four syllables – and we chaps had better get the hang of it. We've been bottling up our feelings for far too long and are the shallower and the worse for that bottling.

There was so much to say to this nonsense that I merely gawped. I was meant to believe that here across a stained and littered tablecloth sat a man who had come to grips with his emotional self, a man who hugged and wept and owned a wardrobeful of appropriate jerseys each with a nice little niche on the sleeve for him to wear his heart on. Here was the developed male, the evolutionary masterpiece ready for all the complexities of the twenty-first century.

I did not believe. Indeed I suspected that if at that moment an emotion had wandered into my lecturer's life he would have shooed it away like a vagrant dog that had cocked its leg over his azaleas, and then retired to his unthinkable study with another cup of instant coffee and a plate of theory.

Nevertheless I said nothing. I did not wish to stretch boredom to the point where I would need to ring for an ambulance. But then he spoke the phrase that acts on me like electrotherapy. We men need, he said, to get in touch with our feelings.

Well, I'm sorry. I don't know who coined this absurd phrase nor do I know why it has gained such currency, but I'm not having it. You see I've had a feeling or two over the years and I've never had the least difficulty getting in touch with them. In fact things have tended to be the other way round – feelings have got in touch with me with unassuageable urgency.

What is all this stuff about the supposed emotional nullity of men? Did this man never go through adolescence? Did he never yield to the horrors of infatuation? Did he never moan and toss and pitch on the ghastly seas of feeling, or do nothing for a month but grunt, or wander alone on the windy hills of grief reciting awful poetry and knowing that no one had ever felt as he? And if he did, does he still say that men need to get in touch with their feelings?

And has he never felt his heart tugged by a work of literature? Has he not gulped for Tess or wept for the death of Michael Henchard who couldn't spell? Has he not eaten the white raspberries of Brideshead or trodden with Laurie Lee the sharp white roads of Spain? And if he has does he still say that men need to get in touch with their feelings?

What does the man and so many like him mean? What does he seek? Does he wish us to blub our way around the world, our lower lips perpetually trembling? Does he believe, furthermore, that all that is felt is equally worthy and that all that is felt should be said? And does he discount all the glittering wonder that springs from emotion kept in harness? Has he no time for the sharp and bitter edge of comedy? Or is he just trying to please women?

So many questions, all of them rhetorical and none of them, I'm proud to say, given voice. I reined them in. I bottled them up. I did what I am not supposed to do. And when shortly afterwards I thanked my host and took my leave I carried them away with me into the welcome cool of the night and when I felt that I was almost out of earshot I screamed the lot of them to the silent sky in a single protracted note. And then I laughed. And then I felt good. And then I went home.

Roosters redundant

My two roosters crow and fight and preen and strut and mount their mothers and their sisters. My roosters are beautiful and useless. No one wants them. In their uselessness they tell the story of tomorrow – the future is female.

On any farm most male animals are slaughtered young. Roosters are macerated by a machine that should be called Herod. At present we have no Herod for the human species, but neither shall we need one. The engineers who will put paid to the human male will be the genetic boffins. Boys and men are doomed.

Genetic engineering has broken all the fences. It is now careering across unmapped territory. The future is easy to imagine but hard to swallow.

The boffins could already clone people. They could engineer an infinite sequence of nice girls who would not crow or fight or strut or preen or bicker. And it is inevitable that they will.

The fate of males is evident in my roosters. To be rid of them I advertised them. I should of course have killed and eaten them but I have a girly heart. Only two people rang. The first was a man who has acquired a rooster to use as an alarm clock, but he isn't happy with it. Apparently it says the cocka-doodle but omits the do. He asked if my roosters did the do. I said that yes, they did the do. He said he would take the prettier one – a Golden Wyandotte.

The second call came from a woman who has a few acres of land. At the far end of her paddocks lives a colony of roosters. The neighbouring farmer used to keep chooks and he let nature take its course which meant that his roosters fought for supremacy. Those that lost had to pack their bags. They took refuge in a distant stand of macrocarpas where they now live together in peace because they have no hens to fight over nor purpose to live for. They peck for grubs and seeds and huddle in the branches at night bragging about the past, watching television and listlessly discussing rugby. And that, boys, will be us. There will be no need for us. We will have scienced ourselves out of a job.

Men are redundant. A few might be kept on in guarded reservations to be milked for sperm to keep the gene pool fresh and bubbly, but with cloning there will be no need even for that.

A few other specimens might be bred and kept to do manual labour. But we will be sterilized and supervised and locked up at night. And we shall have no cause to complain. We screwed up. We fought and shouted and trod on each other. The women told us to grow up but we did not listen because we had muscles. If we could find no one to fight we drank beer and bought war videos and played snooker. We've been out to grass for years but we never noticed.

Time was when we did everything. We did the science and wrote the books and ran the businesses and made the money and farmed the animals and played the sport. Women, we said, could do none of these things. We were wrong. The twentieth century has proved us wrong. And in proving us wrong it also proved us to be useless except as donors of sperm. And now the twenty-first century is ready to remove that sole remaining purpose. Our extinction makes clear rational sense.

We evolved to fight in the endless war of evolution. That war is over. Killing will stop when we stop. Crime will stop when we stop.

The neat irony of this is that we men also built religions. It is as if we knew we were bad. The most durable of those religions extolled qualities like tolerance and peace and harmony and loving our neighbours and sacrificing ourselves for others. These are not the things we do. These are things women do.

We pictured a heaven where the good things happened. We called it utopia which means nowhere. We did not believe that heaven could be made on earth, but it can and it will. The women will make it. It must happen. It is called progress and as we have been telling women for centuries, nothing can stand in the way of progress.

The women of heaven will not seek to grow rich at the expense of others. They will care. They will live on solar power and recycled yoghurt. The world will turn green again and the football paddocks will be planted in soya. Fish will swim, birds will fly. Only gentle things will happen. Endlessly. It will be bloody boring. Cockadoodle do.

Sod scoff

I don't believe in Sod. I scoff at Sod's law. Indeed some months ago I wrote an article mocking the common belief that anything that can go wrong will go wrong and at the most inconvenient moment. I even made a special trip to the zoo expressly to poke a stick through the bars and to tease the great Sod itself. I called it impotent and I called it imaginary.

And then I turned and strode away, ignoring the superstitious muttering of the other zoo-goers, who fingered crucifixes as I passed and buried their nostrils in lucky heather from the gipsy. Behind my back they tossed propitiatory buns to the great shaggy Sod and whispered to their children that I was a bad bad man.

Well the zoo is closed for the Christmas holidays and the keepers have gone frolicking with their families leaving only a skeleton staff to feed and water the beasts. But I can only presume that the keeper assigned to Sod, overcome perhaps by the excitement of the season, left the door of his cage unlocked and beside it a map of Lyttelton with my house circled in red. Because on Christmas Eve my car went wrong.

All year it has been an obedient car. Though I have fed it only a thin diet of fuel, though I have neither buffed its skin nor brushed its upholstery nor paid attention to its workings, nevertheless for 350 days like some Biblical ass it has borne me patiently and uncomplainingly past open garages and unemployed mechanics. And all the while the car was in league with Sod. Together they were plotting its Christmas Eve revolt.

Something beneath the bonnet of the car squealed for several seconds and then the dashboard became a Christmas tree of little lights. I had seen these lights before. On that occasion, several years ago, I found them pretty and ignored them and the car died within hours. This time I studied them. One said 'At Oil Temp'. 'Exclamation mark' said another. 'Brake fluid' said a third. I thought of opening the bonnet but at the same second as I thought of it I dismissed it. I am not very good at opening bonnets and even if I succeed I stare at the writhing tubes and organs in much the same way as the natives of South America stared at the ships of stout Cortez.

I turned the key and to my surprise the engine restarted. Bathed in the twinkle of warning lights I nursed the car home, all the time expecting Popocatepetl to erupt from my tappet block.

Not only was it Christmas Eve, but it was Sunday. My local garage was shut like an oyster and in common with every other garage in the land it would remain that way for a week. I rang the AA and they sent Derek.

When I grow up I am going to be an AA man. He scours the cooling crust of the developed world like a big yellow saviour. He carries a toolbox of happiness. When he comes into view all grief dissolves. He is the flip side of Sod. He is the automotive Jesus who succours the halt and the lame.

Derek boomed ho ho ho and sat me on his knee and wiped my tears and asked me what was wrong. Within seconds he was hauling from my engine the shredded remnants of a thing he called an alternator fanbelt. Derek and I agreed that I needed a new one. Derek said it was up to me to go and buy one.

'But the car,' I said, 'it's kaput.'

'It will keep going a while,' said Derek, 'until the battery runs down. Now off you go.'

I felt as Hercules must have felt when told that he'd got twelve little jobs to do, but Derek was patient. He explained where I should go and what I should ask for and he even wrote down the engine type for me to show to the nice shopkeeper.

Every time I turned the indicator on as I drove into town I was conscious that I was sucking precious bits of electricity from my dwindling store. But I made it to a shop reassuringly called Supercheap where the assistant looked up my car in a rivetting paperback called *Numerical Specifications for Every Bit of Every Car in the World*. He sold me an alternator fanbelt for considerably less than the original price of the car and he wished me good luck and I bore the fanbelt home feeling like a man of world and I rang Derek and he returned to fit the fanbelt for me and

214

the sun was shining and the birds were singing and the fanbelt was the wrong size.

Sensing a shagginess in the shadows, I tossed it a bun.

Mad as accountants

Have you heard them? Surely you've heard them. The people who claim to be nuts. They say it smugly. They announce it like a badge. They trumpet their lunacy. 'When I'm dancing, you know, I just go mad. Absolutely mad.' They pretend to be ashamed but they invite us to admire their disdain for convention, their rich courage. It is chic to be mad, they suggest, admirable to be *outré*, to step beyond the perimeter fence of sanity and dance to the light of the moon.

Then there are the self-styled artists, the writers, the potters, the sculptors, and especially the painters. The painters are particularly keen on their madness, and the women painters are the worst. It's as if their supposed madness stamped their visa to the country of creation. It validates their canvases. 'My family,' say the women painters with the arch smile implying that their family, oh dear, have got it right, 'all think I'm mad. And I suppose you have to be a little mad to want, you know, to want to paint, to need to paint, as desperately as I do. Yes, I suppose you could say I'm a little mad.'

They lie. The lie makes my teeth grind. I hate it

more than I hate prunes. These people are not mad. They are as sane as accountants and a lot less honest.

Let's get this straight. The truly permanently mad don't know they're mad. Their madness is ghastly and useless. It offers no insight, no worth, no good. Only grief. Madness is disconcerting, wearing, scaring. Most of us will choose to keep our distance unless we've had the ill luck to love someone who has gone mad. Then we try to stand by them and suffer their madness with them and everything hurts for ever.

These days we don't say mad. We say mentally ill. And unusually for our softened inoffensive tongue, the change is right. Mad is ill in the head. And most people who are mentally ill are ill in episodes. The illness comes and goes. The awful cruelty of it lies in knowing that it will come again. The head doctors can't do much. They'll tell you so themselves.

For the rest of us, many will be briefly ill at some time in our lives, depression in adolescence or the menopause or whenever and we'll come right again quite soon under sweet old Dr Time. But none of it is pretty. Madness is never good or brave or pretty.

So why should art and romance have attached themselves to it? Why should those who are evidently well, brag of a tinge of ill health? Why should they want to?

Shakespeare has to cop a bit of blame here. It was he who wrote that 'the poet and the lover and the lunatic are of imagination all compact'. And I for one can remember a time when I believed him. I was a sighing youthful lover who fancied himself ethereal and spiritual but who was rather afraid of bodily contact. I thought it rich to be nuts. I thought it creative to be out of my tree. I cringe to think of it. My excuse is that I was young. I knew nothing. What's their excuse? What's the excuse of the dancers and the lady daubers?

Of course Shakespeare's lines aren't Shakespeare's lines. He wrote plays. His characters said the lines. Shakespeare himself, the poet who out-poets every poet since, was sane as a bank balance. Of the few documents we have with his signature on, one's a will and another's a mortgage, neither of which suggests the madman frothing through the world of men with never a care for reality. He held shares in his theatres. He wrote for dosh. When he'd got enough dosh he snapped his pens and bought a house and took it easy.

None of the greats have been mad. They may have been drunks or fighters, but drunks and fighters are ten-a-penny. The drunken fighting writers who write well, write sober. Take bardic Dylan Thomas, the soak and ne'er-do-well, the idle sponger. He was as sane and sober a writer as you could hope to find the length of Serious Street. He wrote, lord love him, with a thesaurus. You can read the number references in the margins of his manuscripts. And only when the text was done and every page of the thesaurus scoured did he reach for the whisky to celebrate. No madman he, nor did he ever claim to be.

It is one of the myths of our society that genius and lunacy are twins. They are not twins. They are not of the same family. Those who boast of being touched in the head are untouched by anything but the blessing of ordinariness.

The backstreet of books

'I told him he was a fool,' said the journalist.

I asked why.

'Because,' said the journalist, 'he threw in a perfectly good job – pension, promotion, security, the lot – threw it in and cashed up and . . .'

He paused while the waiter arrived with our lunch.

'And what?' I asked.

'And bought a second-hand bookshop. And not even a decent one. It's tucked up some side street visited only by dogs and old women.'

'Not much point in asking how he's doing then?'

'No,' said the journalist, 'there isn't,' and he snorted, and we looked down at our plates. Mine held fish, his a steak in a blood puddle. He pinioned the steak with a fork and sawed at the corner. I watched the fibres tear and ooze.

It's not a rare dream, I think, to run a second-hand bookshop. To spend your more boisterous years wringing money from the world and then to shrink into a quiet street and spend the balance of days among tall walls of books.

The world is too much with us. Walls of books

keep it off. Books are the world at one remove. They are permanent, fixed and safe. They can be beautiful but they can't hurt, not really hurt. The wounds inflicted by reading, the griefs and fears, are theatrical wounds, are pleasant pain.

To sit all day amid old books, while outside the traffic hisses through the wet winter, going somewhere, urgent and frantic. To see the occasional customer, a quiet soul in a drab raincoat who wanders along the spines of knowledge, cocking his head to catch the titles, his nature illustrated by the shelves he heads for.

It is not business, or rather it is as close to not being business as business can be. Most of the authors are dead and so are most of the books. The authors who are judged to be live currency will be taken from the shelves within days of coming in but most will prove to be groats or guineas, no longer current in the busy spending minds that throng the city. A second-hand bookshop is a graveyard of spent passions, and the proprietor is the sexton.

I often visit such shops and I do so in just the same way as I duck into a church. It is a quiet place, a sanctuary. I like the smell and the peace and I like the books.

Today I bought for five dollars the *Selected Poems* of Thomas Hardy. Hardy made plenty of money from his novels but after *Jude the Obscure* he gave up on prose and for the last fifteen years of his life he wrote only poetry. It was his way of retiring from the busy streets. He left the new bookshop in the high street with its bright pile of best sellers and moved, as it were, to the backstreet and the second-hand shop that just gets by.

On the flyleaf of the book I bought, written in cheap blue ballpoint:

Danny
Merry Christmas
Good luck up the Whataroa
Happy Reading
Lots of love
Jackie

If that doesn't make your spine tingle we have different vertebrae. I would like to know if Danny read Hardy up the Whataroa. For some reason I doubt that he did. I doubt even that he took the book with him. But if he did and if he sat with it in the evening alone looking out over the deserted valley he may have found these lines:

William Dewy, Tranter Reuben, Father Ledlow
    late at plough,
Robert's kin, and John's, and Ned's,
And the Squire, and Lady Susan, lie in
    Mellstock churchyard now.

And in the churchyard of the poem the voices of the dead speak:

We've no wish to hear the tidings, how the
    people's fortunes shift;
What your daily doings are;

222

Who are wedded, born, divided; if your lives
  beat slow or swift.

Was there perhaps some similar sense of with-
drawal from the world that drove Danny up the
Whataroa, without his Jackie? And is it perhaps the
same urge that drives hermits into caves, monks
into monasteries, and busy businessmen into the
isolation of a shop selling second-hand books?

The journalist laid down his knife and fork.

'I went to see the bloke the other day,' he said. 'In
his shop.'

'How was he?' I asked.

The journalist mopped the blood from his plate
with a piece of bread and popped it in his mouth.
'Happy,' he said.

The big question

'Why?' I said, 'why?'

He looked at me as though I was single-celled. To be fair he was only the waiter, an underling hired to do the bidding of the boss. But the boss was away hitting his profits round a golf course.

It was not the first time I have fired the question. I have fired it in perhaps twenty restaurants over the years with varying degrees of wonder and vehemence. I have fired it so often because I have never received a credible answer. It is the question of the lone giant pepper mill.

I like restaurants. I didn't go into one till I was sixteen and I've barely been out of them since. Food doesn't interest me hugely but not cooking does and so does not washing up. And so does talking to people I like on neutral territory with a little grove of unplugged bottles to ease the gears of conversation.

For the non-cooking, non-washing up reasons all restaurants are good. But some are better. The best of the lot serve large quantities of recognizable food. The furniture is various, the plates and the prices are of human proportion and there's only one cook. And that cook's a woman.

The waiter tells you neither his name nor that he is going to look after you for the evening. He does not have a ponytail and he does not tell jokes. He does not lie in ambush at the door like a pottle of lard. He does not simper after coats and jackets, nor does he address the customer in the third person and the conditional tense – Would sir care to . . .? – because this sir wouldn't.

The good waiter is one you immediately forget. He does not forget you. He appears by telepathy the instant you need him and at all other times he is somewhere else doing what he's paid to do, which is waiting. If at the end of an evening I haven't noticed the waiter I tip him fatly.

As soon as you enter a restaurant, order a beer. The variety of beer doesn't matter because there are only two – brown and yellow – and they taste the same. The beer's a snout-wetter. Its purpose is to get you through the barren rigmarole of menu and wine list.

Of all the restaurant flummeries the wine list wins the prize. But its florid prose goes unread. Wine is sold only by colour and price. Colour is easy. White is for lunch, red for dinner and rosé for the pretentious who pretend they like it. Price is just as easy. The dearest wines on the list are there only for entertainment. They shape the reader's mouth into a gasp. The cheapest are there as ballast.

It would be more honest and practical if wines were not named but numbered. If, say, five wines were available, No. 1 would be the comically expensive one and No. 5 would be the cheapo. And everyone would order number No. 4.

Then the menu. I have written before about the vaunting absurdity of menus but it hasn't done any good. Tiny meals continue to be described in monstrous paragraphs. Drizzling goes on, as does grain-feeding, vine-ripening and no end of nestling.

But in the end the are-we-having-starters debate has been delicately raised and settled, the wine's been unplugged, some food has landed, minds are beginning to mesh and all is set to fulfil the purpose of restaurants, which is to increase the sum of human happiness. Enter, with waiter attached, the lone giant pepper mill. And driven by fury, puzzlement and impotence I fire my unanswerable question. Why?

Why can I not be trusted to pepper my own food? Why can pepper not be treated as salt? Why is the pepper mill so vast? Why in Italian restaurants in particular is it the size of a totem pole, except in Italian restaurants that happen to be in Italy? Why is the waiter allowed to judge the size and location of the shower of pepper on my plate?

The answers I have received have been risible. I have been told that that's how it's done these days. I have been told with staggering redundancy that it is because some customers don't like pepper. I have even been told that it is a way for the waiter to bond with his customers. I left that restaurant unfed.

So when I fired the question last night I did so without hope. I was merely venting my fist-clenching exasperation. But then, last night, at long long last, I met with honesty and sense.

'Why,' I said, 'can you not just leave pepper mills on each table?'

'Because,' said the waiter, 'the punters nick them.'

The tip I left him was a metaphorical kiss.

The man was a pornographist

I wish I'd been the student who stood in Tiananmen Square and stopped the tank. It was all so right. The place, the time, the elevated camera angle, the way the tank manoeuvred to avoid him like some sort of lumbering Dalek, yes it would have been lovely. I wouldn't have wanted it permanently, of course. The idea of a life in Beijing trying to come to terms with bicycles and chopsticks is quite unthinkable, but how sweet to have been flashed around the world as a lone exemplar of heroism, to be wept over and venerated by an army of liberals in the West with their cheap Chinese-made underwear, their raffia place mats and their soft-boiled politics.

I know a woman who was teaching in Beijing at the time and living in a flat the size of a wok about half a mile from Tiananmen Square. By some bizarre bureaucratic oversight her state-sponsored flat had been furnished with a telephone. One morning the woman's husband called from Cambridgeshire, England to ask her how she was coping with the massacre, and she said what massacre, and he said the one down the road, and she said oh and at that moment a trio of her

228

students came crashing into the flat with cheap underwear held to their skulls to stem the bleeding and she said oh *that* massacre.

Of course there's lots to say about that, tedious stuff about global villages and instant communication, but by far the most important question is what was her husband doing watching CNN in the middle of the day when he could have been playing golf or buying place mats or whatever it is that husbands do when their wives are away.

Of course he'll reply that he was watching CNN *because* his wife was away and trouble was obviously brewing in Beijing like that inexcusable tea they favour over there, but I'm afraid that won't wash at all. If he was that worried he should have gone to China with her or chained her by the leg to the vacuum cleaner back in misty Cambridgeshire.

No, I'm afraid the man was a pornographist. All CNN watchers are. Nevertheless on the pyramid of wickedness they sit somewhere near the basement. The pinnacle is reserved for those heroes of contemporary journalism, the foreign correspondents, standing there as smug as Oscar-winners in their flak jackets in front of a hillside on which decorative puffs of smoke appear from time to time as the local heathens battle it out in the traditional manner with remaindered Cold War armaments. Then it's back to the hotel with the camera crew for a snort of manly brandy and a three-course lunch before planning tomorrow's raid on vicarious danger to titillate the zillions in the distant suburbs of Safetyville.

There's a splendid scene in some novel by Tom Wolfe in which a news room bemoans the shortage of good street violence in today's bulletin and sends a couple of cameras out to make things happen. It takes about ten minutes to start a riot among the grievance-loaded dispossessed, all of them hankering for the chance to lob a few stones at society's uniformed prefects. Perfectly legitimate fun, of course, but if it hadn't been for the cameras they'd have quietly lain around the back alleys being hopeless as usual.

And there's no need to shoot more footage of kids throwing stones in the Middle East because there's miles of that stuff in the vault already and nothing's changed. Nor have the comments of the watchers in suburbia who all wonder what the stone-chuckers' mothers are up to allowing their urchins to wander the streets with pockets full of bits of ruin to biff at the riot squad. Well, that's an easy one. Thanks to CNN, BBC, ABC and all the other vultures it's now perfectly easy for the said mothers to stay at home with the telly on and keep an eye on their offspring.

Meanwhile the urchins are having a lovely time, whether they're in Belfast, Seoul or Gaza, playing the local version of cricket with equipment supplied by mother earth. In my teenage years I'd have loved it too. Nothing gave me greater joy than throwing things. The school let me biff the javelin, discus and shot, all of them former weapons of war – though I do wonder quite how effective the shot was – and our aim on sports day was always to try and hit an inattentive official, but how much more fun it would have been if we'd been doing it for real and we'd known that the world was watching instead of a mob of bored teachers with clipboards who were pining for the pub.

Anyway, most of the places that were fighting when I was a kid are still fighting today – perhaps because they like it – and CNN's made lots of money out of them and us.

They don't own nothing

I like to spend money on my dogs but I can't find much to buy for them. A new collar every couple of years perhaps, sometimes a lead. They don't thank me for the lead. They don't like leads. They like freedom. They like the world and they like novelty. I admire that.

I buy them food and it pleases them but there is no point in buying them fancy food. They like crude bones with gobbets of meat and fat and ligament buried in the crevices. They can work at these gobbets, applying extraordinary force to the task by pinning the bones with their paws, gripping with their precise and deadlocked teeth and hauling with the massive muscles of their necks. I like to watch them. They do not care if I watch them or not.

The dogs' lives depend on me. They would find it hard to survive in the wild because game is rare and if they attacked farm animals they would be shot. Each night when the dogs sleep they do not know what will happen tomorrow. They curl up owning nothing. As far as they know there is nothing for breakfast. Every tomorrow is an adventure which starts afresh.

They sleep in my bedroom but if I slept in the garden they would sleep there too. On cold nights they curl in on themselves and generate prodigious warmth. They sleep in the same fur on hot nights and cold nights and they smell only of dog. They drink only water.

In the morning they do not know whether I will take them out. When I do they rejoice. The hills always thrill them.

When nothing is happening they sleep. They sleep lightly and wake on the instant. D. J. Enright wrote a poem called 'The Poor Wake Up Quickly'. It isn't much of a poem but I've always thought well of the title. It's pure dog. And when the dogs wake they stretch, luxuriating in the strength and lissomness of their flesh and guarding it wisely. They tend to their bodies with their tongues and teeth but they never clean the house. If they are sick they sometimes eat it back up.

If I went away and did not return they would pine briefly, but they would not cling to my memory. They would attach their affections to whoever fed them. If their new owners treated them worse than I did they would not make comparisons. They would be less joyous but they would not fret. They would expect nothing, hope for nothing and accept the good bits with relish.

When they are ill or damaged they make no complaint. They curl and lick and wait to get better. They do not imagine what will happen if they do not get better. They do not dread.

Theirs is the state of most creatures on the planet.

It is a state of unknowing. It is a state of acceptance. It is not humanity. They are not vain and they do not accrete possessions. They do not consider themselves better or worse than others. They will fight if they have to for their territory or their food, but they prefer to warn enemies off. They pay no attention to tomorrow.

Though people often personify them, dogs do not lose their dogness. They are incorruptible.

My dogs and I spring from the same process of evolution. In them I can see a lot of where I came from and a lot of what I retain. And I can see what I have lost by being human. I can see the bad bits of the bargain. I can see the crippling effects of self-consciousness. My dogs are my touchstone, my rock of comparison.

Many of the qualities we love to see in people – loyalty, modesty, zest – are exhibited full time in the dogs. Many of the things that we do not like to see in people – duplicity, greed, malice – the dogs are innocent of.

That is why I cherish my dogs. And because they are beautiful. And because they appear to love me. One of them has just come to nuzzle my elbow. I read him these words and he wagged his tail. But had it been a story of abuse that I read him, he would also have wagged it.

He has a bad leg. Some years ago the front bumper of a car smashed it. The vet put it back together and it served, but now it has gone bad again. He carries it off the ground. I have taken him for treatment but the likelihood is that at some time in the next year or two I shall have to decide whether to have his leg cut off or have him killed. Whenever I think of having to make that decision I start crying.

The night of the frozen chickens

I've been asked to speak at a conference. It's the after-dinner part of the conference, when people get down to the business of networking. It's hard and vital work. I've seen many a conference delegate late at night so utterly networked that he's had to be helped to bed.

I have been asked to speak because the conference is about something to do with education and I used to teach. I only taught because I couldn't think of anything else to do but that didn't seem to bother the organisers. And anyway, as I say, it's an after-dinner speech so I don't have to know stuff, and besides the bloke who rang me begged me not to be too serious. Inject a little levity, he said. I said I'd try.

Today I got the letter confirming the engagement. It told me that instead of a fee I'd be getting an honorarium, which is exciting because I've never had one before. Then it went on to tell me what the expected outcomes of my speech would be.

Now I've had a bit of experience with outcomes. When I was at teachers' training college, where I worked hard on my networking but on little else, the authorities were fond of outcomes. Outcomes were the opposite of inputs. We teachers made inputs and the children came away with outcomes. Of course teaching doesn't work even remotely like that but those in the business of teaching teachers have to pretend that it does in order to suggest that they know what they're doing. But any teacher talking of outcomes is usually talking tosh.

And the same is true of speeches. I recall, for example, being asked to speak at a fundraising function in aid of a rural tennis club. The expected outcome was polite applause and a richer tennis club. Quite how it happened that the outcome was me hurling frozen chickens at the audience in the hope of braining a fat man at the back, and that most of the chickens were intercepted in mid-air by an athletic contingent on a social outing organized by the society for the partially deaf, and that in response to the barrage of frozen chickens I was subjected to a reciprocal barrage of beer glasses, and that I put the chicken box on top of my head and ran from the stage peering through the handles in the box while glasses thudded against its sides, and that a woman in the kitchen wiped the chicken blood from my shoulders and then thrust me into a cupboard and shut the door, and that as a direct consequence of my speech the entire rural community was involved in a dust-up which continued cheerfully into the small hours, would take more than my allotted 800 words to describe. All I will say is that it made me perpetually suspicious of talk of expected outcomes.

Such talk presumes that the world is consistent and humanity predictable. That neither statement is true I for one give thanks (though on the Night of the Frozen Chickens my views might have differed).

So much for outcomes. But the letter of engagement was not yet done. Here's the fourth paragraph in full: 'Please give consideration to Treaty of Waitangi and gender equity issues when you are preparing your presentation'.

Now I don't wish to appear ungrateful but I do want to ask why this request is made. In one sense that is an easy question to answer. The conference is being run by a quasi-governmental organization, and I presume it must pay lip-service to the orthodoxies of the age before it dishes out the honorariums. The author of this letter is merely saying what she's obliged to say. Her words mean little more than 'yours sincerely'.

But if by some unlikely chance she meant them, well, I'm sorry. I shall give no consideration to the Treaty of Waitangi nor to gender equity nor to any issues whatsoever when I prepare my presentation. Indeed I doubt if I'll do much preparing. All I shall do is to try to make the audience laugh. And if they laugh it will be because I've said something true. Truth always makes people laugh. And at the same time truth makes all the vapid language of the bureaucratic world seem as hollow as it is. The world will not be tamed by pieties. The world indeed will not be tamed at all, not by me, nor by the government, nor by any platitudes intended to ensure that the takers of umbrage can find none to take.

I prefer to act by sterner judgments of what's right and wrong to say. If what I say is right the audience will laugh. And if I get it wrong then let the chickens fly.

Iguana hallelujah

No one could like gorse. It proliferates like, well, gorse, and chokes whole hillsides into barren nothing and not even goats will eat it. Goats chomp cheerfully on clothing but gorse defeats them. Gorse has mean prickles and a verminous, vertiginous rate of growth.

And yet the flowers of the gorse bush smell sweeter than roses. I know no better smell. As a rule I am not big on smell. All it does for me normally is to take me back to bad things – like the smell of a certain disinfectant which reminds me of school corridors, and of cabbage which reminds me of school dinners – but the smell of gorse flowers fills me with a sort of ineffable yearning. And yet the plant is pestilential.

Contrary and incoherent seem to be the words for this time of the year when winter tries to cling on with skinny talons while the spring is thrusting through in the form of lambs and eggs and sometimes brilliant mornings. Nothing coheres. It is hard to make sense of anything, to try to pull a strand out of all the incoherence and construct a something that holds together. When the world seems bitty and random, when devil gorse smells like heaven, when the seasons are uncertain and the washing machine is on the blink and I smoke too much, nothing seems to make any sense.

Every day I seem to acquire hard nuggets of information that don't fit with anything else, which are like pieces from a different jigsaw to the one I am doing. I am told, for example, that half the adult population of Sweden sings in amateur choirs. What am I supposed to think about that? The Swedes, who have a reputation for blonde Nordic gloom, expensive booze and sexual enthusiasm, spend much of their long winter nights bashing out the 'Hallelujah Chorus' to the Baltic Sea. Why? I don't know. They just do. It just is.

And then there's a student friend who has just been burgled. From the evidence, the burglars toured both the bedroom and the living room of his flat – but not, perhaps wisely, the bathroom – and then they left having stolen, well, nothing. The owner of the flat feels humiliated.

I suggested that perhaps it had been a couple of gloomy Swedes, bunking a choir rehearsal and since they couldn't go home without meeting disgrace for letting the nation down, they just broke in for fun and then got cold feet, not that you would think that they would, given their climate, get cold feet that is. But it didn't cheer him up.

None of it makes any sense. It just is. World, said Louis MacNeice, is suddener than we imagine it. It is incorrigibly plural. MacNeice was subject to dreadful fits of depression and you can see why. If nothing hangs together, if the jigsaw remains perpetually scattered on the kitchen table with some of the pieces upside down and others skulking in the dust under the fridge, no wonder MacNeice got gloomy and headed for the grog cabinet.

Whenever I start thinking about oddity I remember some Mexicans in a desert. I had taken a party of schoolkids to Mexico to have their pockets picked and scan a few ruins and watch a bullfight and sneak into bars to drink elaborate cheap cocktails, and we were crossing the desert by bus, somewhere between Mexico City and somewhere else and there was nothing there except heat, when the bus suddenly slowed and stopped. The bus driver opened the doors and invited us to step out. There beside the road under a single straggly tree stood several women and children in rags. Each of the children had an iguana on a string. For a few pesos you could have your photograph taken with an iguana on your head. The iguanas were dying. The children caught fresh ones every day. My kids took the photos, paid the money, got back on the bus and left the women and children and lizards in the desert waiting for another bus.

There were no houses for miles, nothing but hard-baked desert. What were they doing there? They were waiting for buses. They were poor as could be. Call it economics. Call it anything you like. It won't make any difference. They were there and may still be there and it just is and there's the sad end of it. It fits with nothing, which is to say that it fits with the Swedish singers and the

242

phantom burglary and the sweetness of gorse and the depression of MacNeice. Impose a pattern on it all if you wish, but it would be false to do so. Tough to take, this incoherence. Hard to be burdened with a consciousness in an unconscious world that just happens and does not cohere. The human condition, I suppose. Hallelujah.

The thyroid of Unks

I'm going to become a doctor.

This afternoon, you see, I was fool enough to pick up a ringing phone. I listened for a bit and then I said no.

'Sorry,' I said, 'I can't, not now, I'm busy.'

'Busy?'

'Busy,' I said, 'I'm going to bed.'

'It's two in the afternoon,' she said.

'And I'm going to bed.'

'Why?' she said.

'Because I like it,' I said, 'and because I can.'

'So when are you going to write this stuff?'

'Oh,' I said, 'sorry. I didn't quite grasp your meaning. You mean I should forgo the siesta that more enlightened societies consider a matter of national duty when the heat squats heavy on the hills and the dogs pant in the shade and when anyone in anything approaching a condition of sanity retreats into the deep cool of a shuttered bedroom, I should forgo, you say, that rich and luxurious pleasure and instead should sit sweating before a screen and a desk fan in order to write 500 words for you for some hideous brochure advertising

244

an event which I would attend only with a ring through my nose, 500 words furthermore for which you are planning to pay me nothing but a flitting thank you. Have I got that right? Is that what you meant?'

'Yes,' she said.

'Fine,' I said. 'Okay. And then tomorrow when I am good for nothing because of a shortage of sleep I suppose I am to take sustenance from a few lightly grilled thank yous with a side salad of insincerity, tossing the remnants to the skeletal dogs. Is that what you rang to tell me?'

'I think you've got an underactive thyroid,' she said.

'A what?' I said so vigorously that the dogs retracted their tongues and lifted their heads in wonder at my expenditure of energy on a sweltering afternoon. 'A what?'

'An underactive thyroid,' she said, with the smug calm of someone who has read a whole magazine on her own without help and hardly mouthing the words at all as she read. 'It's quite common. Unks has got one.'

'Unks?'

'Unks. My uncle. It makes him tired in the afternoon and it makes him irritable and it makes him fat.'

'I'm not fat,' I said.

Silence.

'I'm not very fat,' I said.

'Fried food,' she said, 'beer. I bet you barely touch fruit from one end of a week to the other.'

'I find it hard to fry,' I said.

'Your antioxidants,' she said, 'where you do get them from? And think of the free radicals. You're a time bomb. The big C is lurking round the corner. You treat your body like a dog.'

'But I'm nice to my dogs,' I said. 'I let them sleep of an afternoon.'

She hung up. I lay down. But she had banished sleep. I could sense my thyroid snoozing. I could hear the slow clogging of cholesterol. I could feel the creaking of the arteries like hosepipes left out in the sun. I felt the dangers of a little knowledge bearing down on every side. And it was there in the hot discomfort of my enseamed bed that I decided to become a doctor.

It must be so easy now. No doctor needs to know a thing. Any patient worth his aspirin comes to the surgery with a headful of medical mysticism garnered from that fount of all hocus pocus, the Internet. All the doctor has to do is to agree. That wild yam cream, yes it's just the thing for those phyto-oestrogens. That selenium supplement, a bonzer idea. Zinc for the prostate, absolutely. Ginkgo, you can't go wrong. Your thyroid, as underactive as a dozing Spaniard.

Has there ever been a time when so many lay people have claimed some understanding of medicine? Has there ever been a time when so much simplistic nonsense has been spouted about health and so much credulous attention paid to it? Have we lost sight of the truth that the body is a massively complex entity and that most of our tinkering is little more than faith healing? And have we forgotten that the body is intrinsically robust, and that if we run around a bit and eat a bit and laugh a lot the body will see us out for an appropriate number of years more or less regardless of what we do to it? Have we ever been so hypochondriac?

I don't know, but I do know it's a good time to be a doctor. All I'll have to do is roll up for a couple of hours each morning to stamp my official approval on the diagnoses and the nostrums of my patients. And that will leave the afternoon free for something that actually does me good.

Up the Pope

You've got to hand it to the Vatican casting agency, the College of Cardinals or whatever they call themselves. They've got it right this time. That Pope of theirs, he's just divine.

They've promoted a few bozos over the centuries but this one's a corker. Being a Pole helped, of course. Poland's spent its history freezing and being invaded and has sought solace in potato vodka and mysticism. The result is that martyred soulful stuff that just can't be bought.

And what names the Poles have got. They spend their first three years at school learning to spell themselves, which sets them off on just the right footing, showing them from the outset that nothing's headed their way on a plate. It's a recipe for success we in the West have forgotten with our extraordinary nonsense about self-esteem and our frantic terror of death and dingoes. A good dose of hardship in the formative years and the ills of prosperous decadence are cured at a stroke. Expect nothing and life's a breeze.

But there's more to the Pope than Poland. He's talent. He's a natural. The cameras love him. And he's just gone on getting better. Look at him now. Frail, vulnerable, posture gone, legs going, spine like a question mark, body raddled with old bullet wounds and a voice like a coconut husk. They give him stuff to read out in twenty-seven languages and he speaks it straight into the ground and makes it sound like a bus station announcement on a wet afternoon but the crowd goes nuts.

He's a star. He's up there with old Nelson M. and Desmond T. and Ma Theresa. It's that goodness rap. It works. You just can't buy it. It beats looks. It beats sex. It beats youth. It's strong. Put the Pope in the publicity ring with Schwarzenegger and in a matter of seconds old abs-and-pecs Arnold is flat on his back and gulping like a fish. This goodness caper, it's power.

The church needed this pope. The twentieth century had bashed the church up. Science had it in a throat lock and the old ecclesiastical moves just weren't working any more. And even though the science boys may favour bad clothes and thick spectacles, they know how to turn out someone telegenic when they need one. Old Einstein was a cracker, all mad hair and mid-European opacity. The seething congregation of tabloid-readers hadn't got a blind idea what he was on about but they were used to that. Having listened to the mass in Latin for a millennium and a half they were ready for something fresh. Curved time and the fourth dimension hit the spot. $E = MC^2$. Who knows what it means? Who cares? It sounded just funky.

When Einstein cashed in his chips you might have

thought the church would seep back into the gap but the brain boxes had a fresh gun in the armoury. They wheeled in Stephen Hawking. He looked like something that ran a planet in *Star Trek*, all shrivelled body and thunderous throbbing brain. The crowd went wild. Everyone bought his book and didn't read it. It lay on coffee tables throughout the West like a profession of faith.

The thing that Albert, Steve and old John Paul have got in common is that for them the flesh seems to matter less than the other stuff, the big stuff, the life of the mind, spirit or whatever you want to call it. The temporal is nothing. They transcend the temporal. And we love it. It doesn't matter which of them is right, indeed it doesn't seem to me that right means very much in these circumstances, although it does to some people and they will write me incandescent letters. But what does matter is the shared disdain for hairbrushes, holidays and exercise equipment.

The Hawking star has faded of late but John Paul's just won't stop rising. Now he's off round the Middle East dogging the steps of St Paul, although on his road to Damascus he's swapped the sandals for a brace of Pratt and Whitneys. But when he lands, that soil-kissing stunt is a beauty. Every time he goes down on his knees it looks like it might be for the last time. Apparently the bodyguards are bristling with winches and defibrillators. But there's still juice in the old boy, or I'm a Platonist.

Then he goes into solemn apology for the evils of yesterday while a covey of plump cardinals bob around and fret about diplomacy. But he doesn't fret. He just hoes in, wearing the inviolable armour of simplicity and goodness. He won't make a jot of difference to the local fanatics and their cherished ancient feud, but he's doing everyone else a treat. He gives us the strange in the ordinary. He gives us more than the body. He gives us the frail man with the big inner light. We need it. We love it. It's good and it's us.

Would you care to?

'Dancing,' she said, 'there will be dancing.'

'Oh good,' I said. 'Will there be country and western dancing led by a man with a stetson and a microphone whose ignorance of cattle-ranching is matched only by his ignorance of English, chanting bizarre instructions in an accent and a jargon that I can neither understand nor pardon to a group of people dressed in check shirts, bandannas and embarrassment? I do hope so.

'Or failing that,' I said with a fervour that I found hard to hide, 'is there any chance of a throwback bash for the middle-aged, giving them a chance to fling their bald spots around to the songs of long-dead adolescents, songs whose lyrics have the emotional complexity of crockery but which the oldsters can remember to the last syllable, an achievement of which they don't seem in the least ashamed? What fun that will be. A couple of hours and the baby boomers will be telling spectacular lies about the swinging sixties that swung for everyone except them and then they will gather in grinning circles to perform an activity called the twist which will lead directly and promptly to a local citizens' petition to build an enlarged spinal unit. Groovy.

'But if not that, then perhaps you're running one of those lovely formal balls that recall a more gracious age in which the music is supplied by a spindleshank dance orchestra and the costumes by a museum? Those attending will have prepared for the event with a month of evening classes run by a haggard woman from Wainoni with a fake Hungarian accent and grey, wispy hair clenched into something called a bun – though if you sank your teeth into this bun they would bounce.

'And while the dancers lurch around the floor, the fortunate few who have managed to sit out this particular dance will be divided neatly by sex. The women will coo and melt and mutter how it takes them back to the days of elegance when courtship was civilized, men were gentlemen and groping was what you did for your teeth in the morning, while the men will say nothing at all because they've long since snuck out the fire exit, their hips a-bulge with flasks of relief. Is that the sort of dancing you have in mind?

'Or maybe you mean to stage a truly modern dance event involving a condemned warehouse, a couple of turntables, an illiterate DJ in laughable sunglasses, a skipload of illicit drugs and a pullulation of teenagers? The girls will be wearing short skirts of net curtain over the top of trousers, like a valance round the legs of a bed, while the boys will sport canvas cargo pants whose crotch sits snugly at knee level.' (Such low-slung trousers may be a fashion statement, whatever that may mean, but they are not an athletic aid. A friend of mine was recently attacked by a group of youths in such trousers. They hit him a bit so he ran off, and though he had half their lung capacity, twice their years and three times their paunch, he got away with ease. He said it was like being chased by pygmies in shackles.)

'If,' I said, 'it is this sort of rave dancing that you have in mind, remember that it not the music itself that matters but the level at which it is played, that indeed the volume and in particular the bass must be of such prodigious intensity that the noise is not heard but rather felt. And remember to truck in a container of narrow cans of caffeine and sugar concoctions known as energy drinks, so called because they have supplied energy in abundance to three hundred advertising agencies who have got into the profitable business of conning the young into buying them.

'Or maybe,' I said as a thought struck me, 'you are planning an evening of performance dancing, in which we watch either women of improbable fleshlessness tottering around the stage in a bid to inflict terminal damage to their toes while pretending to be swans in a fairy story put to music in 1860 by an unlamentedly dead Russian, or else, best of all, a programme of modern dance for us to watch in which men and women intertwine themselves inexplicably in a sort of space-suit pornography to music that sounds like a leaking outhouse. What larks,' I said.

'Actually,' she said, 'I was thinking of a disco.'

'Oh crikey,' I said, 'what more could I wish for? A chance for me to relive the humiliation of my teenage years, when everyone was supposed to like dancing and while it was all right for the girls who could jig pointlessly on the spot, it was firmly not all right for the boys, of whom two were gifted dancers while the rest of us were deeply and permanently incapable of any movement that didn't look self-conscious, contrived, demented or simply the quintessence of jerkdom.'

'You're not really into dancing, are you?' she said.

You too

We've all heard it said that everyone has a bore in them, and the plain fact is that it's true. Everyone does have a bore in them. But it's no use just talking about it and putting it off till you've got a bit more time on your hands. There's only one difference between real professional bores and people who fancy that they might get round to boring some day, and that difference is that bores bore.

Bores don't waste time telling people how they are working hard on boring and any day now they'll burst on to the boring scene with a dazzle that will throw all other bores into invisibility. No sir, true bores just go right ahead and bore. To be sure, they don't get it right all the time but the only way to learn to bore is by boring.

That's the tough news and I thought I'd give it to you straight. The best thing you could do now is to put this book down, buttonhole someone and bore them. You'll make mistakes but you'll also have made a start.

Your first hurdle is your natural modesty. You've seen great bores in action and you've stood in stupefaction and wondered how anyone could be so boring. You may not have said so in so many words perhaps, but somewhere in the soundless reaches of the soul you have felt it. You could never be that boring.

Well, take a moment to reflect that the bore who so arouses your wonder was once a demure uncertain fawn not unlike yourself. Hard to believe, I know, but he once doubted his opinions, deferred to others, thought listening was a virtue and worried about what other people thought. Like you he was weak. Like you he had no fun at parties. But since that date he has gone on a journey of discovery and so can you. Each one of us, be he never so lowly, has a bore in him, and don't let anyone tell you otherwise.

And indeed that is perhaps the nub of it in one sentence: don't let anyone tell you otherwise. Indeed don't let anyone tell you anything.

When you first try to bore you will trawl your mind for something to be boring about and come up with an empty net. Don't despair. You are just fishing too deep. Go to the surface of your life. You need look no further than your children. They make perfect beginner's boring material. If you are childless, pets are just as good. I began my own career with dogs.

As a nervous beginner you will feel the need to arm yourself with facts – an early hero of mine could manage a full hour without digression on medium density fibreboard – but as you grow into boringness you will find yourself discarding facts as a porcupine discards its quills. A bore does not have to know things. He only has to say things. Manner, in short, is greater than matter. Dogmatic certainty is everything and facts are nothing.

For example, I have no idea if a porcupine discards its quills but so long as I state it emphatically and allow no interruptions I can bore. If your technique is sound, people will shrink from trying to correct you, just as you shrink from correcting the bores you so admire.

From then on the joys are unlimited. You will become a connoisseur of boring. Remember always that a bore is a body as well as a voice. The good bore uses his body like a sheep dog. Even while he is boring he is quietly guiding his victim into a corner, nudging him by imperceptible shifts of the feet until he has him pinned against the fridge. Then he uses his arm like one of those barriers at army camps to block the only route of escape.

Eyes matter too. As a good bore you must always look straight at your victim. He feels obliged to meet your manic gaze and so cannot scour the room for help.

To begin with your victim may try to contribute to the conversation. 'Ah yes,' he'll say, 'that reminds me of . . .' Quash him instantly and hard. Reduce him to expressions of agreement only. If these are not forthcoming, insist on them. 'Am I right or am I right?' is a phrase that all bores master. It works unfailingly. You can sense your victim slump.

When his eyes finally fall to his feet and he swirls the dregs in his glass and watches himself dig the toe of his shoe into the carpet and swivel it about, you know you've got him. It's a lovely moment. Once you've found the joys of boring you'll see social functions in a whole new light. It is more blessed to give than to receive.

Bedside lovers

I cannot imagine not reading. Some books, of course, are like lovers; you go to bed with them once and fall asleep immediately. My bedside table is piled with such books, which I have started but will never finish. They lie face down in heaps, frozen open at an early page, like a stack of dead moths. Sometimes a stack topples and the books lie for months on the floor, their spines permanently deformed.

But other books become house guests. They take up residence in rooms of the mind and never leave. If I sit quietly I can hear the footfalls of several authors in the grey and looping corridors of my head. Albert Camus pads around up there in his suit, smoking Algerian cigarettes and never smiling. On his way to the bathroom he passes a fat, smug Evelyn Waugh and doesn't even nod to him. None of the authors, indeed, pay any attention to each other. But each can sing and each has sung to me.

The books which have lodged in my skull I read mostly between the ages of sixteen and twenty-two. I have heard people say that character is formed by the age of seven. They may say true, but thought is formed later, I think, and so are some forms of sentiment. These writers soldered the wiring of parts of my mind, such that there are times when I feel with their fingers, think with their words, tap my toes to their rhythms.

I do not always recognize the debt, but sometimes when I say a phrase or think a thought I hear a grumble from a distant room, and I realize that the phrase or thought is borrowed from one of my house guests. So I go to my shelves and pull down the book and sink back into its world. I soon forget to seek the line I had echoed and am absorbed by the hypnosis of the language. It is like pushing open the door of the pub and seeing an old and dear friend at the bar with an empty stool beside him and a full glass.

So it was recently. Something took me back to Laurie Lee, and I spent the day reading *As I Walked Out One Midsummer Morning* for perhaps the fifteenth time.

As always I found something new:

Eating bread and sausage, my back to the church wall, I was aware only of this point in time, the arrested moment of casual detail, the unsorted rubbish of now. I felt the heat of the sun dampened by draughts of ice blowing from fish-boxes stacked nearby. I remember a yawning cat – a pin-cushion of teeth and whiskers – sitting on a palm-leaf in the gutter. A man said 'Good morning' and passed out of my life, stepping on a petal as though extinguishing a match.

*

That scene lasted a few seconds. But sixty-five years later I can see the man and his boot and the petal more clearly than I can see anything in this dusty room I am writing in. I can see it indeed more clearly than if I were shown film of it.

But the phrase that matters is 'the unsorted rubbish of now'. We live in a dump of detail, a welter of tiny nothings, of heels descending on petals and of cats yawning. They make no sense. They are unsorted rubbish. It takes a Laurie Lee to sort the rubbish, to transmute it into permanence, to make a false, seductive coherence out of what does not cohere.

A while ago I had my ears syringed. As happens every year, they had become plugged with wax. My hearing had dulled. I had adjusted to the thin trickle of sound that squeezed through. When I emerged from the surgery, sound assaulted me. Rain beat a tattoo on an awning. Car tyres hissed like cats. I caught bites of conversation from across the street. Through the open window of a pub I heard a woman talking about the death of a horse.

Reading can do something similar. It can syringe the ears, ream the nostrils, scrub the fingertips, scour the tongue and peel the eyes. I cannot imagine not reading.